A PICTURE OF HEALTH

by

Constance Hardy

THIS BOOK IS DEDICATED TO MY FAMILY

WITH LOVE AND GRATITUDE

ISBN 9512046 0 2
Printed by Waterside Printers, Blanefield

Available from
Heatherbank Press, 163 Mugdock Road, Milngavie, Glasgow G62 8ND

CONTENTS

Scott House, Edinburgh Academy, circa 1902

CASTLE IN THE SKY

I   LOOKING OUT AT A WAR

Our nursery window looked out over green playing-fields. Beyond this lay a public park, neat avenues of trees bisecting grassy football fields, and halfway up in the sky, the magnificent cut edge of Edinburgh: Arthur's Seat to the left, plunging down over Salisbury Crags, and then the climbing hill up to the Castle on its knob in the middle. To the right, domes, towers and steeples. That window seemed exclusively mine, although three older sisters and our barely older aunt had shared the same riches.

Across the playing-fields moved an old man behind a mowing machine drawn by an old horse which was wearing boots. Slowly, they made satin stripes on the grass, east and west, all summer long. When the horse relieved its pressures, the old man trudged forward with a bucket which he filled with his hands, and replaced it on the mower handle; then the two of them continued their measured tread. In the summer, the horse sometimes wore an old straw hat with two earholes. To the right of the field was still an untended piece of rough grass and spinney and a slow little stream, with an enlargement called the Beetle pool. On warm afternoons, this held the whole world in it if we lay with our noses at water level. Caddises heaved along the sodden leaves at the bottom, and water skimmers and boatmen whirled around the top in a wild freedom. A picnic beside it was an adventure.

These years were spent during the First World War, and there was no freedom indoors at all. Home was a school boarding-house

1

of thirty schoolboys. In the sundrenched early years of the century, they had grown up in the spirit of freedom if not its practice. Their group photographs hung along the walls, stalwart young men with moustaches, arranged in rows, their bulging forearms folded right over left, left over right on either side of the housemaster, his wife, his family, the matron, the housetutor, the houseman, and the house dog, Jack, who looked like the original terrier of His Master's Voice. Jack won fame later as his barks were reputed to have disturbed a group of suffragettes who were trying to pour petrol through our letterbox to set us alight. They went on and created a fire in another school instead, this protest aimed presumably at the training of male chauvinists. Behind this arrangement of strong men, children, and dog, stood a row of seven or eight stiff maids in waisted black, aproned, with caps and streamers. Were these ever pulled off on a rowdy night?

By 1915, all that had gone, the maids to make munitions, the oldest of the moustaches to battle training. We were reduced to one maid called Lizzy, of short wits, with cracked glasses frequently mended at the bridge with darning wool. She must have worked prodigiously, and never stopped singing a dirge called "I'm the Black Sheep of the Family". I think she was an orphan. The boys were asked to polish their own shoes and Army Corps boots and to make their own beds, which brought out a chorus of protest by letter, from worthy mothers, many of them Colonial wives still with batteries of native servants, who were horrified to their Scottish souls by such a hint of effeminacy in their young. Our patient mother tried to convey to them the home situation, but they were unconvinced.

Our father became a Special Constable, and, on top of his teaching and other responsibilities, had to disappear several times a week looking very splendid in bluish-grey uniform, on a horse. Food became difficult: the boys lunched in school, but morning and evening and weekend meals had to be both filling and heating, and rationing was strict. We were a bread and bun nation then: potatoes, turnip and cabbage the only remembered vegetables, occasional cooking apples and rhubarb the only fruit. Oranges appeared at Christmas, and at Sunday School treats, when we went off for the day with a bag of food, and a tinnie — a mug tied on with string, to receive hot sweet tea out of an enormous urn. We ate rhubarb jam from our own patch for two years, *never* on margarined bread, until we discovered our neighbours had gooseberry jam from theirs, so we did a swap. We kept hens, which all caught croup, and one of my sisters nursed them all, dosing them with whisky as they yawned and croaked in the laundry. They survived, but it was a long time until spring gave them the impetus to go egg-laying again. We also had a domestic rabbit warren, but the discovery that one dinner dish was actually Flopsy gave me a life-long scunner. Cannibalism would be preferable — or did cannibals jib at eating friends?

One dietetic oddity not forgotten was my sudden discovery of a jar of capers on the top shelf of the larder. Their sharp taste seemed delectable, and I can remember scrambling up a set of slate shelves to steal them, getting stuck at the top, and shrieking. Another shrieking match, still clear before ageing eyes, was the sight of a polar bear coming out of the linen cupboard opposite the nursery door as I was going to sleep. Too many capers perhaps. Nightmares were frequent though. My long straight hair was twined with rags that tugged to make it look nicer in the morning, so I often had to sleep with a buried nose. The war stories of men and horses dying at the front in drowning mud gave, and still give, appalling claustrophobia and dreams of rich horror. I often woke screaming, and an adult would eventually appear. Recurrent earache was put down to 'tonsils', which were removed on the dining-room table, under gas and oxygen, some years later.

Indoors was gloom. I can still see the sinister pages of *The Scotsman* and their effect on Father. In close black type were hundreds and hundreds of names of dead and missing in the battles of the Somme and Passchendaele. In four years of slaughter, thirty-eight boys who had lived with us and with whom he had worked and enthused, died, many straight from the classrooms or the rugby pitch outside. He thus lost thirty-eight sons, and only had four daughters of his own. This was far worse for my older sisters, but if it had not been for a pillar of a nannie who had been with us for years and who kept life aggressively normal, living might have been very different. Mornings in the

3

park, or learning to read with her, afternoons at the Beetle Pool, and always, conversation. She was my rock.

If things went wrong with personal life, her solutions, — "It will all be the same in a hundred years," or "Worse things happen at sea," — straightened them out. But when we had to sing "For those in peril on the sea" after naval battles, it was with convulsive sobbing. Another comforting statement, in response to demagoguery, was "Too much jaw, dear". This comes to me every time I see a sociological jargonist with wagging beard and earnest glasses impressing his theories on the masses. No theories for her; just common sense and practice. Later on in life she continued this. When I came home from school, cold and desperate, she'd be by the kitchen fire. "Come and have a nice piece of fried bread, dear." It always worked; peace and stability reasserted themselves.

One night in 1916 a Zeppelin appeared, and the whole household retired to the cellar. For the first time, I saw boys in pyjamas and longed for such sophisticated garments. When we came up to daylight in the morning, we visited our white mice in the nursery, to reassure them. They lived in a two-storeyed villa with a wire front. It had a living-room, where they ate, a matchsticked runway up to a spare playroom, and, through a pophole, an entirely private bedchamber, full of smelly cottonwool. We were astonished to find that, during the hostile night, they had carried all their bedding through the pophole downstairs to their equivalent cellar, and were already engaged in carrying it all up again. We never had another air-raid warning, nor did they ever do it again.

The houseboys used to josh us if we met them, but seemed a separate race. Later, Nannie took on the role of Matron, and used to love it when they drank her health in their prescribed nostrums, usually beastly, often oily, but I used to grudge sharing her. She was the only one with time to spare, that childhood need. One week, there was a touch of romance. One of her brothers came up to spend some sick leave from the war, with a precious matchbox. It contained a bullet that had been taken out of his leg, and he limped, to prove it. Every wartime Thursday, houseboys who were willing came to our drawing-room to pick over sphagnum moss, which was gathered from the summer moors and sent as padding to dressing-stations, and to knit large, earnest, knobbly khaki garments for the troops. The nimble ones were given socks, and Mother and Nannie turned the heels for them. I can remember two homesick twins quietly weeping, and mopping up with a bit of misshapen scarf. Being young didn't seem much easier than being old then.

Nursery days were punctuated with diseases; horrible earache recurred often, and infections brought home from school. Scarlet fever, measles and diphtheria could still be killers, or leave chronic trails of heart or kidney damage, deafness, or damaged sight, and there were special Fever Hospitals for their reception, to prevent spread. You shouted at the patients through closed windows, and everything they wore or touched had to be burned. Being at the end of the family, I was lucky. Everyone had had everything, so I could stay at home. Measles and jaundice came along together, and so horrifying was the sight of my red face and orange eyeballs that I was thankful to be segregated behind a carbolic sheet at the nursery door, with only Nannie bringing bread and milk, and later a luxurious slime called Calves' Foot Jelly. There were visits from the doctor, a fierce old person with a lot of yellowish-white moustache and booming bonhomie. He thought pain was a bonus and a character builder. At the height of measles, when I was seven, he economised on a visit by renewing a smallpox vaccination which was considered due, and scarred my arm with what looked and felt like a blunt fork. Not unnaturally, this blew up to great discomfort, which he welcomed as proof that it had 'taken'. The scars still prove that it was a thorough job. If you went out you wore a red ribbon round the afflicted arm, to warn people to keep off. Horses which kicked wore the same signal at the root of their tails.

Medicines seemed compounded on a system of the beastlier the better: nothing that tasted good could possibly be good for you. If you had a sore throat, and someone gave you a spoonful of jam, you mistrusted it, waiting for the bitterness likely to be buried in the treat. This condition was generally treated with bitter burning tannic acid, applied with a tickly paintbrush from the nursery paintbox. Painful earache demanded the application of warm oil, or a small hot onion, while toothache was staunched with oil of cloves. These were palliatives, but the doctor had no better remedies, and besides, his visits were expensive. For a bad cold, we had to drink ammoniated quinine, a fiercely bitter draught. Great emphasis was laid on bowel action, which was supposed to occur daily. In nannie-trained households, the child was sent off for this purpose after breakfast, and inspection followed. Inability by the second day meant 'Taking Steps'. Horrific mixtures of senna, hot licorice, or Gregory's Powder, all rich in irritants, were given, and, failing action, Castor Oil neat out of a tumbler in which it slowly and noxiously rolled . All this violent dosage frequently induced further seizures from shrieking insides, and laid some recurring troubles. The reminiscences of Jane and Thomas Carlyle give an admirable picture of this gruesome habit, the importance in their diaries for the need and ingestion of a Blue Pill taking priority over the visits from Leigh Hunt and John Stuart Mill, or even those to Lady Ashburton.

Wartime milk was thin and blue, and collected from the dairy in a can, along with eggs. These, as they depended on farmyard searches in the stackyard, were often unreliable. You had to break each separately before adding it to any mixture, and the horror of rich, flocculent green sometimes revealed when you cracked the Sunday breakfast one was appalling. The curate who reputedly said his egg was good in parts became a reality. Coughs and chest were always suspect. Tuberculosis lurked in the milk, and it was a common thing to see scars in a neck where tubercular glands had been lanced: the high collars worn in adult life were often for cosmetic rather than fashionable purposes. A well-endowed family across the road with whom we frequently played lost three of its members from this disease — a beautiful adolescent, a ten-year-old boy and a baby.

Street lamps each bore a notice saying 'PLEASE DO NOT SPIT ON THE PAVEMENT', and this was endorsed in the tramcars: 'M.O.H. says SPITTING SPREADS DISEASE'. Once infected and detected you were segregated like a leper in a special hospital. The wards had walls the colour of wilted lettuce, the beds in long rows, the only decoration the temperature charts at their foot. The spikey graphs on these were the last thing to inspire confidence, and the general care was often basic and unimaginative. I can well remember visiting a patient after a recent lung haemorrhage. A plate of dry mince and cabbage was dumped on her chest, and, at tea-time, two hardening slices of bread and margarine. No wonder the outlook so often seemed hopeless. One always recognised the ex-T.B. patients from the way they coughed — with head averted and a handkerchief to the mouth to contain possible sputum.

During the war, energy was hard to come by, and we travelled by buses with huge floppy gas bags on the roof. These contained methane. Once the roof bags started falling in on themselves, we had doubts whether they would last until our destination. After them came the cable cars, worthy double-decker trams that churned up and down our steep hills by means of a wire and a ratchet in a slit between their wheels. Some of them had open tops, and rides were exhilarating. On our bicycles, we had to learn to avoid their grooves in the road. Cable cars were superseded by electric trams, with a flexible mast from the roof, reaching up to an overhead wire. They had open decks at either end. The great excitement was to sit here when the terminus was reached, and watch the conductor swing the mast down, walk round the tram clutching the rope, and connect it again at the other end, with a lot of hissing blue sparks. A delectable spice of danger after safe transport.

> "A being that moves in predestinate grooves,
> Not a bus, not a bus, but a tram."

Trams bred trust: they were stable, steady, and went to where they said they were going. They would accept a pram behind the driver in front, and allow the mother and contents to climb in at the back, decanting the pram to the pavement for her at her destination, a civilised and friendly action. The city was also served by a splendid ring of railway. You could ride round the town looking into the kitchen windows, which were much more revealing than the fronts, with food, families, drying dishcloths and a geranium on the window-sill. This was *real* travel.

During these war years, our family members worked in their separate ways. Father doubled as teacher by day, part policeman by night, while Mother coped with the desperation of house-

7

keeping for about forty persons on short commons, with little help; weekend meals were especially difficult.

My oldest sister, at nineteen, worked as secretary in a highly pressured hospital, while the next worked on the land. She went to a Borders farm with a friend, and was shown a tiny bothy to live in. Being asked for the lavatory, the owner genially waved his arm and said, "There are plenty o' bushes aboot." The next sister was still at school, drawing incessantly, in a dreamlike state in which she could lose herself. Without Nannie, I don't think I could ever have grown at all.

Eventually, with the signing of the Armistice in November 1918, our great horizontal skyscape was lit up by fireworks. I can remember King George with his medals and Queen Mary in her tiara and diamonds, quivering in the sky above the black castle, their effigies spitting and blazing against a background of scarlet fountains, golden rain, blue streaks and green effervescence which took its time coming down again, and lit up the park trees with a viridian glare that looked like the pictures of hell in our improving books.

II   TOWN AND COUNTRY

The war that was said to end war brought relief, and incandescent hope. How long did it take to wither? Being sick almost unto death entails the relatively simple matter of surviving, but convalescence is a far more drawn out, depressing, endless affair. Illness used to be a matter of endurance: once fever had passed, the body had slowly to collect its own resources, and climb up the long hill by painfully slow degrees. Whooping cough used to reduce us as children to croaking shadows, and we whooped afterwards every time we had a cold. We were sent on dreary walks round the gas works beside a wet and windy sea, draughts of sulphur dioxide being considered therapeutic, but we came in so cold that we whooped for more hours afterwards.

The same unrewarding tedium attacked the nation. Organisation for returning soldiers was slow. Many jobs which had been taken by women had to be reallocated. Men wanted heroes' lives and heroes' rewards, and these were not forthcoming. Everyone was still struggling and hungry. Many of them had lost limbs, had their lungs ruined by gas, and were mentally shaken by shellshock. At the end of it all, my father's hopes and joys in education suddenly snapped. He tried to end his life in a violent depression, and my mother found him in the bathroom, bleeding. He, she and my oldest sister, another victim of desperate hard work and depression, went off to Canada for a summer, where an aunt, uncle, a ranch, and a lot of horses, with an infinity of quiet space

9

did their healing work.

We moved to a house that seemed to me poky, a mouse house. It stood in a terrace, and had wire guards against the lower windows, with brass rails on top, to stop the neighbours looking in. The only other places where I have seen these were in stuffy legal offices and (I surprisingly learned later) a brothel.

The Edinburgh of 1920 was a city of the Establishment, a pillar of conformity. The four professions that dominated it were the Church, Education, the Law and Medicine. As each considered itself the undoubted leader of the community, they can only be put in alphabetical order.

There were probably many other candidates, but these were the ones we met and, at the risk of being partisan, Education was far the most interesting, partly because it lived all over the city and allowed the odd eccentric to flourish. The Church was spread about too, but Law and Medicine tended to live in their own ghettoes, at least the upper echelons did, generally in districts of total respectability.

The Old Town of the city had hugged the spine of the High Street, running from Holyrood Abbey in the east up to the Castle in the west. It was sprigged with innumerable piled pends and closes and stairways, where high heid yins and hoi polloi had cohabited. Drainage was minimal in the days when the roads were covered by what was tactfully known as the 'Floo'ers of Edinburgh', and as people became 'nicer', they moved to the north, where the wind blew fresh from the Forth. Pet dogs provide their 'flowers' nowadays, the pavements still harking back to earlier days of primitive hygiene.

The legal luminaries lived in the parallel rows of the northern 'New Town' leading off the steep hill descending to the river. There, they were in reach of the Court messenger who delivered their papers neatly wrapped in pink tape. This they called red, presumably under the same principle that a red hunting coat is called pink.

If you walked along the streets of lawyers' homes, a heavy air of correctness flowed out from the treated stone facades and the clean swept steps. Every front door was painted the deep green of dusty holly. This was a 'lasting' colour, guaranteed not to chip.

Above the polished brass letterbox or the polished brass door-bell was a polished brass plaque proclaiming who resided within. The polishing was done early every morning before the postman came, by servant girls in black stockings. Below these doors were basements, protected by spiked railings, often beautifully decorated by Robert Adam's acanthus ironwork. These were guarded by a notice announcing Tradesman's Entrance, a locked gate and another brass bell. When the bell was pulled, a lever was operated in the house to open the gate to the grocer, the journeyman, or a spindly message boy who manoeuvred an enormous shopping-basket down the steps from a bicycle that he had ridden over the cobbles. No one dreamt of carrying home their own messages. These solid granite setts had been laid all over the hilly city to enable the horses to get a grip as they hauled their loads up from the port of Leith. Riding over them by bicycle, horse cab, or car was a bumpy process, and most of them have now been flattened under tarmac.

The Law's windows were usually above pavement level, so that you only had glimpses of dark brown rooms backed with shelves of leathery books and a dim light, often gas, hanging from the middle of the ceiling, but generally the desire for privacy produced the inevitable cream casement cloth curtains across the lower sashes. Any variation in this routine practically proclaimed one a foreigner, who knew no better. A gap in the curtains might reveal an aspidistra, a plant that could flourish in gas lighting, or a face keeking out at the street.

The Edinburgh Establishment produced absolute rules of behaviour. You had to be introduced, then to leave cards. If the family concerned thought you suitable, they returned your own. Following this guarded interchange, visits might follow by invitation. One family returning from India had a large bowl in the hall full of these cards, which were used one day as firelighters by a new little servant girl. As they had no means of checking up on the calling parties, they were ostracised, and no further callers came. Coformity was absolute, and if you stepped outside it, the family name was besmirched. Against this background it was difficult to adjust to changing circumstances, or develop any individuality at all without risk. The rules were set, like the

Catechism we had to learn in Sunday School.

Once we had been officially introduced to the Law, some of its members were generosity itself. We went to an annual dinner with one, who was teetotal. This was fun for us. We had only seen our parents with a glass of port on rare occasions, and had never tasted it. The dear Sheriff concerned was vague as to the constituents of alcohol, but he did know that Christmas pudding ought to be illuminated, so he commissioned his cook to pour half a bottle of violet methylated spirit over it, and ignite the mixture. The same applied to Snapdragon, which we played afterwards, snatching almonds and raisins out of a blazing dish, and eating them, unsurprised.

Another house had two lively sisters, and their brother who had been a judge in India. On retiral, he was taking holy orders at New College, aided by innumerable cups of tea. My father always used to josh him about muddling his Hebrew and his Teabrew. One of the sisters who had been a pupil of Alfred Cortot in Paris used to play Chopin beautifully after dinner. The ex-judge, once ordained, used to preach to the unconverted at the Mound on Sunday nights, where he was joined by a retired Edinburgh Sheriff of the Law Courts. These meetings were then usually religious, but later grew largely political.

The New Town houses were large, cold, and had three storeys and a basement, with attics for overflowing children and domestics. The basement kitchens usually had two deep niches at the back, originally intended for box beds for the kitchen staff. The central passages opened at the rear on to gardens, which were cut into peculiar shapes with their neighbours, like oddly divided cake. There cats prowled and yowled, and only on Mondays the washing flapped. Other washdays were not permissible, and no one went out there on Sundays. The ground floor was mainly occupied by the man of the house and his books. When one character died, well over eighty, his family came upon an upper room piled solid with a neatly folded *Scotsman* representing every day since he had qualified. Lawyers' families lived very formal lives, their good name being essentially important. They kept themselves to themselves, and made others feel like outsiders. It was a known rule that no advocate's wife must be seen carrying a parcel.

When our mother came to Edinburgh as a bride in 1895, she was asked out to dinner to several legal houses from whence came our father's pupils. They went to three in one week. At each was a butler, with white gloves, and the table bore a large central épergne crowned with a plumed pineapple. When dessert was due, the recent bride was asked first by the butler what she would like and she replied, "A slice of pineapple, please." (Her father, a vicar in South Wales, had grown them in a pit.)

"Madam, the pineapple is not for cutting," she was told.

As a bet with herself, she tried this on each time with the same result, and concluded that the butler and his pineapple were a permanent pair.

After these dinners, guests retired to the drawing-room, and were asked if they had brought their music? As if by chance, they had always left it in the hall, and they sang for their past supper. My parents were charming duettists, and lived down the pineapple episode without difficulty. These evenings must have shown progress from earlier ones. In the Georgian houses, the dining-rooms had low panelled skirtings, which contained a concealed cupboard lined with zinc. This was to house the chamberpot, when the gentlemen were drinking together. Our family sideboard had one too, and I was always told it was for leaking wine bottles, which was fairly accurate, I suppose.

Medicine, and its eminent practitioners, lived in a cluster round the West End. There were medical families, like hierarchies, and they intermarried with the regularity of royalty. Their ladies may have been nurses, so the correct aura of reverence was preserved. One married outside her group a colleague of my father's, thus switching her allegiance, considering it a step down. Her air of kindly patronage is still remembered and was passed on to her daughters, who behaved rather like the young ladies of Mansfield Park. There was a son too, but he kept newts in a glass tank, which humanised him a bit. His maternal grandfather was Surgical Chief to the doctor who later married my eldest sister. This pundit knew what he was about, but did not care much for the theories of asepsis, and used to demonstrate this to his juniors by spitting in the wound before sewing it up. Perhaps this humanised him too!

A PICTURE OF HEALTH

All these professional gentlemen had their uniforms. The lawyers wore black coats, pin-striped trousers, stiff white shirts and what were known as 'Come-to-Jesus' collars — two stiff points, parting at Adam's apple, above a white bow tie which would show above their gowns once they reached the Courts. In the streets, this was topped by a bowler hat at the right angle — too much and you were a bounder. The judges wore something larger and blacker. With neatly rolled umbrellas, they walked in penguin pairs up the hill discoursing in their own peculiar phrases in what was recognisably a refined legal voice. The words 'may clayent' often floated back as they passed.

The medicals used the same formality, only their hats were large black Homburgs and the older generation were said to carry a catheter inside the lining band. They journeyed by large and respectable dark-coloured cars, except for one dearly-loved maverick, who used to ride along Princes Street on a very upright bicycle. Fortunately everyone knew him and where he was going, as with no warning he would extend his arm at right angles and immediately cut across the traffic. Status was as essential to these gentlemen as Virtue to their ladies. Of course no doctor was ever seen without his Black Bag: when he was high enough up the medical tree, an assistant carried it for him.

The Church appeared the most unapproachable of the lot. Their collars were so white and gleaming, their clothes so black and well-brushed, and on Communion Sundays, four times a year, they were resplendent in long frock coats to their knees and top hats. Many of them looked as if they were ordained solely to proclaim the Wrath of God, and, as with policemen, our knees trembled with incipient guilt as they passed. Guilt certainly helped me along the directives of behaviour. Psychologists seem to have removed a lot of it, and made life a great deal more difficult for children, who can see black and white, justice and injustice, clearly, but cannot come to terms with the adult's view of grey areas. God was not a loving friend in the streets of Edinburgh; he was a fierce old man carrying a load of retribution under his belt. The bells of his churches clanged in a threatening fashion. Only the Roman Catholics, and these were mainly regarded as dark conspirators, knew how to come to

14

terms with him and could visit his house on other days than Sundays only. They also looked happier going there, and were a much more informal group, allowed to enjoy themselves on Sunday afternoons, after Mass. We could not play or sew, but had to read supervised and suitable literature only.

After war ended, we had a golden month on a Border farm: haystacks to bounce in, an orchard hanging with plums, huge horses on whose vast backs you were heaved, fat legs doing the splits. They tossed their splendid heads, and if you were careless, you got the knob of the hame in your eye. Their shining and deliberate haunches, the colour of a newly-shelled conker, started to strain till the pull of the wagon behind eased, and they just had to lean on their great collars polished black, dangling with winking brass amulets. There was a local show, and their manes and tails were all pigtailed up in red, white and blue bows and pompoms, while Geordie, the horse and orra man polished their hooves and hissed. No royalty could beat them for dignity, and Geordie swelled beside them. He fascinated us, as he had lost an eye in the war and a glass orb replaced it. He would take it out so that we could gape at the glowing red socket, and we thought we could read the slow thoughts in his brain behind. As he lost this eye continually, from straws poking it out, he had acquired a spare set of different colours. The eye that made you behave was a pale blue that winked; the eye we loved to watch was a guessing game, brown on Mondays, speckled on Wednesdays.

That holiday spelled FREEDOM in capital letters, as we were so much with strangers who acted as tolerant friends. The other enviable freedom was that of the farm children, who wore knickers with no bottoms: what a saving of time! Their mothers were 'bondagers' and wore bonnets known as 'uglies', their brims stiffened with rounded canes. There seemed little crying in the country, only tolerance and measured industry. We had escaped from conformity, and the ready tears which erupted when it was flouted dried up for a month. It left a taste of perfection.

Travel in the nursery days was really exciting. A horse and cab would arrive and was loaded with a basket of bed linen and knives and forks, an enormous Gladstone bag full of our father's books which the cabbie could hardly handle, and our own personal bundles for the seaside — jerseys, bathing-suits, sand shoes, a bucket, and, when you were old enough, an iron spade, the sign of seniority. No puberty was as exciting as when you graduated thus, and could leave the wooden one for someone else's nursery. It had the same thrill as first wages. The horse would arrive fairly fresh, but my mother always had a drink ready for him, as he had a long uphill journey ahead. (This was regarded as so unusual that the proprietor actually sent her a letter of thanks.) Refreshed, he would plod up the cobbled hill to the station, which was full of smoke and hoots and puffings and blowings. It was a royal send-off, into the train to the Forth, and across its marvellous railway bridge. Getting over the initial disappointment of not going up and down the arches, but through them, you always had to throw a penny out of the window into the water. There was the river with its islands, especially the little fortified one that supported the middle pier, and there were the shores of Fife. The stations counted off were very special, Aberdour with its castle, and Kinghorn, where you had to mourn poor King Alexander and his horse falling to their death off the cliff; then the air full of the aroma of linoleum. We used to recite:

"I know full well by that fearsome smell
That the next . . . stop's . . . Kirkcaldy."

Next came Largo, where Alexander Selkirk dreamed up Robinson Crusoe, and at last, at last, Elie on its golden crescent of sand.

April in Elie on the first morning was a clarion call. We pelted out to the rabbit-bitten grass beyond the harbour, the air full of the baa-ing of new lambs, the sky trembling with larks, the dunes with primroses tucked in the folds, the empty matchbox clutched in case we found rubies in Ruby Bay, and finally the picnic on ship's biscuits and cheese at Newark Castle, looking at St Monance. No holiday could ever touch that for pure sensation.

We were into the icy sea in a trice, but I was timid. A friend drew lines on my torso with indelible pencil until at last, on a day of triumph, a line round my neck proclaimed that full immersion had been achieved.

In summer, we went to England, a grisly night journey to Bristol, changing at Carstairs and Crewe. Carstairs locked its waiting-room all night, and the remembrance of several freezing hours under a smoky lamp with a bursting bladder is still haunting. Later, we used boats, embarking at Leith after lunch on the Royal Scot or the Royal Fusilier. There was a first class, fairly respectable, and a second class where we got all the smuts from the funnel. We gazed at the coast till darkness fell, about St Abb's Head, and went to bed in bunks. Waking with no land in sight, we felt like Vasco da Gama, but by dusk we were opposite Tilbury, pausing for the Thames pilot, and watching for the dangerous manoeuvre of his navy blue legs reaching for a ladder from a boat rocking from the wash of other marine monsters. A stoker came on deck and reminisced to us. When the real pea-soupers descended on the river and no guiding lights could be seen, the pilot steered by smell, he said. The coffee dock, the sugar dock, the banana dock, his nose sniffing like a dog's took the ship creeping up the river safely until suddenly Tower Bridge loomed, and we moored in the Pool of London. What an arrival! Into the bunk again, and in the glittering morning we landed beside the Tower and plunged into the thrills of the Tube. This ship's exercise cost £1.50 in 1920, as we always carried our food with us, partly for economic reasons, partly to avoid the dining-room in a rough sea.

The return journey was made from Bristol. Plunging from the respectable heights of Clifton down the Blackboy Hill, where the little black slave boys used to hug the dogcart rail behind their tobacco-trading masters, we embarked on the Avon in the middle of the city. We rather sneered at the Avon and its glaucous mud, as we had heaps of real sand in Scotland, but peering up at the Suspension Bridge, Mother would tell us of the love-crossed lady who had climbed the railing to plunge to her doom. However, the wind had filled her crinoline, and floated her down to the mud, where she stuck and waited for a bedraggled rescue. (She died recently, a respectable old lady.)

At Avonmouth, a ship that had grounded unloaded its cargo of over-ripe bananas on the bank, and a ghastly miasma of sick syrup filled the air. Once into the Severn, we bunked down and awoke to turmoil; the Atlantic and the tidal races were meeting and quarrelling at St David's Head. The only antidote to this gastric upheaval was to nibble plain chocolate, and suck a lemon.

There was beautiful Wales on the right and beautiful Ireland on the left to look at, and by afternoon we were in Belfast to off-load cargo. Then there were three hours for foreign travel on a tram ride round the city which always seethed with children. Re-embarcation was followed by one of the most beautiful land-falls ever, the entry to the Clyde in the dusk, Ailsa Craig with its knob, Cumbrae with its hump and Arran with its jags, a bunk again till morning, and a train from Glasgow. I forget the economics of this journey, but it has made air travel tame by comparison. Years later, a patient in my husband's medical practice was asked where she had been for her holidays. "I dinnae ken," she replied. "I flew."

Sometimes we spent August at Newtonmore, then a less known Highland village where a College friend of our father's had built a house in a firwood. A bungalow then was a novelty; the excitement of having no stairs, but rooms opening off a big hall, a gathering place after long days on the hill, or swimming in the Calder where it ran fast. Among the firs grew the red toadstools with white warty spots pictured in all the fairy books, and we made gardens of them, which rapidly decayed and stank. An uncle from Canada made a wattle hut in this wood, where we could take a book and teatime bannock, or listen to the whispering pine-needles, and sometimes see a slithering lizard making for the warm stone wall. I still remember that smell of dry conifer, and outside and beyond, the mats of waving bog cotton, the patches of rich bog myrtle which we took home to scent the blankets, the call of the curlew crying over a further horizon. Holidays were extra special then: we could be alone, and shout, released from having to keep quiet in a small house with a study in it. The period of mourning for all those war-lost young lives hung over us for years.

My father was a man of tremendous enthusiasm, all of which he poured into his teaching, and aged pupils still remember the high spots. Having taught Classics and realising early that they were not to the taste of all, he plunged into vivid Italian for some of the less motivated. We were told, just by chance, how memorable was a spaghetti-eating contest — who *can* have cooked it? — accompanied by Italian expressions descended from the ancient Roman tongue. On another occasion, he illustrated how to lasso a steer, using a high stool (certainly stationary) and in History, he became an ancient Pict brandishing a weapon (his ruler) at the invading hordes under Hadrian. It would have been far more satisfactory for us to sit in his class, rather than at the meals later, when he was reduced to monosyllables after the exhaustion of so stimulating those resistant to learning.

My earliest remembered contacts with him were being taught the Greek alphabet, aged four. I can still repeat it, but can't read it. Later, I carried his golf clubs round the Royal Burgesses course at Barnton, where one opponent was an elderly man wearing a scarlet Burgess's jacket and Dundreary whiskers, whose equipment consisted of two clubs and one ball — a brassie for driving with and other purposes, and a putter tied to his waist, which he swivelled round for use on the greens. With minimum equipment, they went round in about 6 over par for the course, and at home we had a series of competition toast-racks and mustard-pots to prove it.

The best times with him were occasional walks on the Pentland Hills from Balerno to Carlops or to the Fishers' Tryst pub; these were the only occasions, alas, when real conversations took place. On one we took a future Rector of Edinburgh Academy and a future vicar of our church to have a look outside Edinburgh, and we all buried lemonade bottles deep in the Cairn on Cock Rig.

III   NISI DOMINUS FRUSTRA

Edinburgh's civic motto is Nisi Dominus Frustra. Dominus for us stood for a dominie, a figure understood, a respectable gentleman. If you kept to the tramlines, and did not strive in vain, he would not frustrate you.

Admirable as this theory was for a way to get along, it did reduce enterprise, and tended to produce a tamed lot of children. If you stepped out of line, it reflected on your upbringing, and brought the parents into disrepute. No wonder we screamed, and ran like manic hares in the freedom of the holidays. Conforming children were still seen and not heard in public, so that conversation was conducted on conventional lines — on 'goodness', whether school was liked or disliked, what was liked best there. Although these were questions, they were all rhetorical. If you said you did not like what you should have liked, the conversation faded or you were ignored, as when you were asked what you would like at tea, and bypassed the bread and butter stage by asking for a biscuit. This applied to the period rather than the circumstances as far as I was concerned, as our parents were desperately involved in their smothering responsibilities and my sisters were a lot older.

Life therefore did not pose philosophical questions, but facts. A Scottish education was based on facts: tribal customs labelled you, as did the clothes you wore. The enviable splendour of a girl who wore bronze dancing sandals with crossed elastic over

20

neat white socks resembled a mixture of Miss Rockefeller and Scarlett O'Hara. As she was the vicar's daughter (he had a rich wife) and an only child at that, such a state seemed unattainable. Coming at the end of a family of three sisters and the aunt who had been reared with them all, I inherited my clothes fifth-hand, made to fit after a fashion. Several winters there was a scratchy red coat that grew shorter and shorter, and a black beaver hat with a tight elastic under the chin. We were once taken to the zoo, and a monkey thrust his hairy arm through the wire, seized the elastic and went 'ping'. I thought I had been guillotined. Mother used to put things away so carefully that they sometimes disappeared. This happened at last to these hated garments, and I was freed from itch. To guard the legs and feet we wore boots and leatherette gaiters. Boys' boots had those convenient hooks, but our inherited ones had little holes through which we had to push laces which had always lost their bound ends, and gaiters had to be buttoned up with a hook. What weather was it that we were all so terrified of? Waterproofing was in its infancy, and if our layers got soaked through, cold and fever lay at the end usually. One must never sit on wet grass; someone's little girl had done so, and died. The city had always been called 'east-windy and west-endy', and we seemed perpetually to be meeting both hazards.

Grown-ups wore long, dark clothes, and their skirts might be edged inside with fuzzy braid to scatter the dust. This had to be brushed out after wear. I can remember a dog coming up to Nannie. "Dear Doggie," she said, loving all animals, and he wagged and used her skirted column as a lamp-post. Once in a Princes Street shop, standing beside a long-skirted grown-up, I walked out of the shop with it, only to discover it was the wrong one. My bawls soon brought rescue, but it was terrifying at the time.

Hats were always worn out of doors, and often in, especially if you had guests to lunch. They looked like ceremonial platters, and many ladies took pleasure in trimming their own millinery in ingenious fashion. My mother shamefacedly confessed that she often had inspiration during a sermon. Ladies of a certain age wore lace or veiling over their necks up to chin level, stiffened by little white posts sewn in to keep it upright.

Men still wore stiff collars, and layers of stuffy clothes that smelled of tobacco, or worse. The air was very dirty then, and dust was everywhere. Edinburgh was not called Auld Reekie for nothing, and dry cleaning was almost non-existent. Wash days were major affairs, requiring a laundry, a laundry-maid, a boiling copper, countless tubs, a mangle, and eventually a mammoth ironing bee. The Lower Orders, as they were then called, often wore clothing cast off by their masters, and were usually smaller. You would see granny, mother and daughter, each generation growing slightly taller, and with straighter legs. Granny might well be bowed like a croquet hoop from childhood rickets. The children played in the street, knitted scarves wound round their chests and pinned at the back with enormous safety pins. They wore large and leaky shoes, if they had any, and their noses were yellow with snot. High above, from the tenement windows, their mother would yell, "Hi Jeannie, come wey up and get your jeely piece."

Against the gloom, there was much jollity, spontaneous rather than pub-induced. The maids sang at work, and many of the workmen, so you learned a lot of words not met in middle-class conversation, and naturally their company seemed much more interesting. The maids were always capped and aproned; a coloured morning frock, and respectable black for afternoons. If you met one in her nightie you had no idea who she was. The workmen were fortified against the climate in cloth cap, vest, flannel shirt, long-johns under their trousers, a jersey or two, an apron, an old jacket, topped with a heavy overcoat for going home in. The surrounding atmosphere thus became rank. No one went bare-headed. Everyone was afraid of catching cold as it might be followed by such savage results, and until washing was easier, the workers' next-to-skin woollen vests stayed on all winter, day and night. The tram going up the hill of the Mound to decant the Infirmary out-patients had a smell so thick that one often puffed up the hill on foot in preference. Vistors to the hospital had to stand on the pavement, often for over an hour in the rain, waiting entry. I wonder how many new patients were created in this manner?

Class was clearly distinguished by dress, so one could sum up

occupation and social level. There were astonishing embargoes on
who were asked in to play, and who not. To the professions, Trade
was something not quite nice. This was even fiercer in the
Southern University towns. An old friend, the daughter of the
Master of a Cambridge College, said that Gown was never allowed
to meet, or play with, Town. Being an unathletic and asthmatic
'intellectual' daughter, she yet had the prerogative in the Gown
games of choosing the teams, as her father was Master of a Very
Senior College! Thank goodness, we managed to choose our
friends: Nannie was not overcome by the proprieties. She liked
interesting children.

Games were either rowdy, or respectably quiet: children were
still seen, but shushed, so as not to be heard. An aunt from a
parsonage wrote in her diary of wild heterosexual games of
hockey, cricket, tennis and bicycle golf with her sisters, visiting
curates and their friends, but such gaiety had ceased by our day.
Once out of the nursery, girly girls and boily boys were different
races. We did unite again at dancing classes, where you bowed or
curtseyed to your partner. These were great occasions of good
manners, which many of us badly needed, coming out of segregated households. Apart from 'figure dances', when one was
a Flower, thudded through a Scarf Dance, or caracoled in a
'Housemaid's Dance' — (which engendered Nannie's scorn as,
after miming sweeping dust into a dustpan, we then waved it
in the air upside down) — we learned Foxtrots, slow Waltzes,
and usually ended up whirling in a riotous Polka. One beauty,
now vanished, was the Lancers, with its eight different figures.
We are only left with the Eightsome Reel for mixed relaxation.
The dancer in the middle leaped high and whooped if a boy, but
did neat chassées with held out skirt if a girl. Dancing classes
always ended with a procession in single file, 'walking gracefully'.
The girls curtseyed and the boys bowed to the teacher, who
acknowledged them with elegance. There was no monkeying
about.

Parties were limited to the Christmas period, or possibly other
girls' birthdays. Drawing-room games were of the Pass the Parcel
kind, or progressive competitions where you each had two minutes
at different exercises and totted up marks. You wore a party

frock, carried your indoor shoes in a bag embroidered 'Slippers', and ate sandwiches, iced cakes, jellies and blancmange. Sometimes you had to sing, or give a party piece, but generally showing off was sternly discouraged. Nice little girls were part of the background.

Parties were a change, and therefore something joyous to contemplate, but frequently flat to participate in, occasions when the frenetic jollyings of female parent, innumerable aunties and perhaps one rash uncle failed to galvanise us. Perhaps we were blase, but were always game for Charades, when our inner life had a chance to escape.

The children who played in the streets made their own fashions and we might follow them, if we had the skill. Hoops, skipping variations, ball bouncing against a wall with interminable rhymes that formed a ritual, whipping a wooden peerie with a piece of string that interfered with people's feet, playing marbles in the grooves of the cobbles, and diabolo, a great test of skill — whirring a sort of enlarged waisted cotton-reel on a cord between two sticks, tossing it high in the air and catching it again — all these succeeded each other, season by season.

At one stage the little 'street girls' became highly domestic, crocheting huge shawls from tiny rainbow ends of wool. They would sit in the basement areas on kitchen chairs, with flashing fingers, little mothers of the future, a fine example of industry which was unfailingly pointed out to us.

The streets themselves were far livelier and dustier then, with more deliberate traffic. Milk, coal, goods, cabs, were still horse-drawn. The milk horse stopped at the right doors without a murmur from his master, who still took a pride in blacking his hooves with boot polish. The coal horse was stronger, sadder, and less well kempt. He used to heave a cart full of hundredweight sacks up the slippery hills, his masters hoarsely shouting their wares. It always seemed to be raining, the men were usually sodden and had empty sacks over their carboned heads, against which they would lean their great loads and totter up the flights of tenement stairs. An awful day's strain for man and beast — every house and single-end had its coal fire, and a small enough bunker to store it. Fishwives strode along on pillared black legs, with striped petticoats, shawls, and great creels on their backs, propped by leather snoods against their foreheads. They were magnificent women, with a great pride in their husbands' catches, which were glitteringly fresh and sold from door to door. Each had her own round, on her own day when all the family expected fish for dinner.

By the pavement edge were buskers, street singers, a blind man with a fiddle or mouth-organ, an old Italian lady on an invariable route with her barrel-organ and donkey, sellers of matches or bootlaces who were often returned but jobless warriors. The high spot was the one-man-band, with cymbals on his knees, a drum on his chest, bells or a clapper at his elbows, and pan pipes fixed under his chin. The children danced to his music in the street. On the pavements, artists would draw brilliances in coloured chalk, sunsets, roses, and in the tourist season round the Art Galleries by the Mound, tartan gentlemen with couthy sayings written below. After the pubs came out, though, all these delights were better avoided; sights and sounds lost their charm.

Quiet games covered a wealth of writing and drawing. Consequences, Picture Galleries, Word and Question, Heads-Bodies-and-Legs, Poetry Competitions, Paper-Doll Dressing — they all gave head and hand a lot of practice, and some ferocious talent surfaced in most unexpected areas. Autograph books among the girls produced correct clichés, or occasional outrage. The energetic kept diaries with 'SECRET' on the front. We respected this, but irreverently reading later those of the game-playing aunt, we discovered that any faintest hint of romance — touch, glance, quiz, smile — was immediately rendered in French. The vicar's daughter, she commented, "This afternoon the lawn is black with curates."

To us, this was forbidden territory. Anyone developing heart throbs had to keep quiet about it. There were clear conversational embargoes: Religion, Sex and Money were never discussed. Love was too often mixed with Duty, which made it dull. This probably saved everyone a lot of trouble, but caused difficulties later, when the beauties of the marriage state and bed were considered Duties, which took away a great deal of spontaneity. If a marriage went wrong and went as far as divorce, the lady, willy-nilly- was ostracised, whatever barbaric behaviour her spouse may have indulged in. A friend of my parents, whose husband was knighted after their parting, took on his title, and there was great shock as this made the situation ambiguous.

Social functions outside the home occasionally involved invitations to the Pantomime at Christmas, with a statuesque Principal Boy, the famous Florrie Forde, nodding with ostrich plumes and the most adequate silk-clad thighs imaginable, or to a Picture House, the flickering film assisted in sensation by a lady at the piano playing 'suitable music'. This preceded the wonderful Wurlitzer organ by years.

Near us there was a 'common picture house', where entry to the two front rows immediately under the screen was allowed in exchange for jam jars or rabbit skins. Alas, we were never allowed to test it.

For family events, well-known friends came calling again, leaving two cards, one turned up at the corner. In later years, a cache of these in Mother's effects were found kept faithfully, and some bore the damning words "To congratulate you on the birth of your fourth dear little daughter". No wonder I loathed dolls and longed to wear pyjamas. Fortunately, an older male contemporary, who was a lot richer, cast off his toys, and the rapture of a pogo stick, a pair of stilts, and a battered motor where I pedalled furiously under a dented bonnet, are remembered highlights. Later in life, he initiated me into mischief in their cellar, where he had discovered that if you fixed a string to overhead wires you could make the doorbell ring, and one of his sisters who was awaiting a suitor dashed discreetly to the front door. We fell about laughing at such inventiveness.

Before the twenties, babies, who had always been born under a gooseberry bush, rode about on their nurse's arm for their first months. A 'monthly nurse' came to the house, where the mother was always delivered, and where she was not allowed to stir for the first weeks. The medical fraternity was terrified of haemorrhage or embolism. Mother was cherished and given Baby at three-hourly intervals, until Dr Truby King said it should be four-hourly only. Eventually she could make the sofa, where her husband kissed her hand and close friends could come and congratulate or commiserate. You had a maid then, who said you were 'Not at home' when you manifestly were, so that you might pick and choose. Later, the official nurse either arrived or took over baby care with the aid of a nursery-maid if there were other children.

Nurse proper was often clad in navy blue serge from head to foot, wore a little velvet bonnet with streamers, and looked like a bishop off a chessboard. Once the baby went out, it was covered in white net like a plate of meat, and carried through the dusty streets. We lived near the beautiful Botanic Garden, but at that time handbags and umbrellas had to be left at the gates in case rare horticultural specimens were smuggled out in them. For many years this ban extended to prams and go-carts, and what couldn't one have smuggled out in a baby's long clothes, worn for nearly six months? They were a woolly vest, a bodice, a barracoat made of flannel and decorated with feather stitching, a cotton petticoat, a dress, a jacket and an enormous shawl. No wonder these infants always appeared to grizzle; they must have lived in a permanent state of thirst and sweat rash.

When too heavy or lively to carry, they graduated to a pram, a sort of high-wheeled gig, and nannie status was judged by what you wore and what you pushed. Our nannie, having joined our family in 1904 at the age of eighteen and trained in the rich book of experience only, was rather a lone bird. She was the oldest of ten children, and knew a tantrum from a trick. She had a low opinion of toffee-nosed nannies who depended on appearances. "All show," she said shortly.

I inherited a rather rickety go-cart in which I was pushed, and from which I was once removed to ride home in triumph in a motorcar, while Nannie had the demeaning experience of shoving it home with a battered teddy bear as occupant. The bear was fifth-hand like my clothes: he had lost one eye and his grunt, after being left out one night in the rain, but he was deeply beloved, and when they gave him to another child with no toys when I was eight, I was heartbroken.

Nurses, when they met, used to conduct hissing commentaries on the Goings-On in their headquarters. Our nannie barely listened, and never opened her mouth except for a crisp aphorism. I can still remember hearing of one mother — don't look now but listen — whose troubles were Drugs and Drink. These were obviously worse than Death or Disease, and I speculated on what she-devil could possibly be found. One day, I was pushed into her room by her children, and a dear warm little creature clasped me to her padded bosom, smelling strongly of peppermint, with a delightful flush and a ready laugh. I thought she must be a very cosy mother to have, and, as she never seemed to leave her room and there were always chocolates there, probably she was too. Her children loved this situation, but the nurses sniffed.

PISKY HABIT

IV   MANNERS MAKYTH MAN

Marriages, the next event, were led up to gradually. Unless a
gentleman inherited money, he had to have enough to keep his
bride in the state to which she was accustomed, and this had to be
earned. He was therefore usually older. One heard that A was
seeing a lot of B; concealment was impossible as the female circles
met over tea-tables and notified each other with nods, becks,
wreathèd smiles, shrugs of approval, or the awful silence which
implied a doubtful future. Marrying out of one's class, for instance
— at least downwards — was unthinkable. It entailed not being
'out of the right drawer'.To the infant eye, loving rapture did not
come into it, rather a shared interest in parental profession, tennis
or golf. A young lady mught go out to India for a season, in a
group irreverently termed the 'Fishing Fleet', and capture a
beautiful young man in spotless jodhpurs. One devastating story
was told of a groom who, having come home, had perforce to do
a lot of walking, so that his Cavalry calves swelled. As he waited
in his Regimentals for his bride at the altar, he was seized with
terrifying cramp, and his kilted brother, who was his best man,
had to snatch the skean dhu from his stocking and slit his boots for
him. How the indignity was lived down I have no idea; probably
the well-bred congregation ignored it, and the couple passed out
under the guard of honour of crossed swords, smiling into the sun.
When about eight, I was included in one of these wedding
invitations, and afterwards attended the reception, where all the

presents were laid out. This rite, and the number of your brides-maids, was the status symbol for you and your parents. Prowling up and down the table gazing at the procession of silver entrée dishes, with curlicued lids, plated egg-boilers, and at least eight pieces of glass with silver filigree on which you were supposed to stand the breakfast teapot, I could see not a single article worth coveting. At last I found one, a gift of the bride's brother: a clock-work mouse. (He showed further acumen by eventually ending up high in the Civil Service.) While the bride changed afterwards there was a lot of sibilant discussion on where the honeymoon was to be spent, but it was said to be a total secret. Timbuctoo? Xanadu? LONDON? Expectation rose and rose, but once they were off in a hail of rice and old shoes, all was revealed: it was to Gullane, twenty miles along the coast, where there are four golf courses!

The weddings, or rather pre-nuptial celebrations for the working classes looked really exciting to the outsider. If the bride worked in a factory, she was dressed up in a bit of veiling and some splendid glad-rags with a bunch of flowers, and then paraded through the streets near her work by her mates, either on foot or in a horsedrawn cart. Everyone shrieked happily, and the pièce de résistance was a large china chamberpot carried ahead, filled with coarse salt, a sign of fertility. This was tactfully omitted when obviously unnecessary.

Deaths were a different matter. Sometimes long-expected, and even anticipated by the road outside being bedded in straw to quieten the traffic, when they occurred blinds were drawn and no-one emerged until mourning clothes had been assumed, from hat to shoes and gloves. The loved one was said to have 'passed on', or the word 'died' might be changed to 'deceased' which was less crude. It was strange that this, an experience one spent one's life being prepared for, always appeared veiled in ambiguity. At that period, with deaths in infancy, childhood and adolescence more frequent, and taking place usually at home, it should have been a natural maturing process for the whole family, but the strength thus gained was not allowed to show.

Children's literature was full of early and holy deaths, and we were reared on a thumbed copy of *Ada and Gerty, or Hand in*

Hand Heavenward. The house that we moved to in 1920 stood on a street that passed a large cemetery, so that funerals were frequent. One heard the clopping of horses' hooves, and rushed to the window. According to income or importance, either two or four magnificently plumed black horses with foam-flecked chests harnessed to splendid bowed necks by a bearing rein so that they could not rush it, drew a glass hearse, decorated with rich black carvings and two top-hatted gentlemen on a box. Inside, the flower-covered coffin lay like a jewel, sometimes covered in purple felt, sometimes made in oak with fine brass fittings. Not too rarely it was small and white, and you knew that this might be Ada or Gerty, and reality drew nearer. A convoy of carriages with similarly restrained horses passed by, with gentlemen dressed in full mourning. Ladies did not attend. Then silence, and rumination; but sometimes I had to go out with shovel and bucket for the horse-droppings for the garden. In one of our children's papers, one boy asked another what he was collecting the dung for.

"To put round our rhubarb."

"Oh, we put custard round ours."

The simple humour of the time.

When seven years old, I was taken to see a dead grandmother, a kind and serene old lady whom I had only recently met. It was too much that this warm woman who had actually praised me should be corpse-cold. This took a very long time to get over.

Church was an institution, both parents having been raised in the beauty of holiness. My mother was one of twelve parson's children who had shared a crowded, disciplined, but hilarious youth in South Wales. My father was more strait-laced. His parents had gone through the beginnings of the Indian Mutiny together, until his father, in the Lancers, had managed to send his wife away by ox-cart. In the charge of a faithful havildar and an ayah, she rode from behind the lines to Bombay, a toddler at her knee, and suckling her newborn baby at one breast and the ayah's babe at the other. (The poor creature had had no milk.) They saw her safely to the ship, where she caught smallpox and they all had to be quarantined, but eventually she reached home. After this, the mercy of God was never away from her lips, or from the impassioned letters she and her husband were enabled to exchange

31

and it stayed as part of their lifetime foreground. The lack of relaxation showed in their eight children, a very individual bunch, two contiguous brothers growing up into an Anglican monk, who was also a writer and a painter, and a delightfully bawdy bachelor who became a naval captain. Possibly as a protection, rather than an act of favouritism, they were referred to in Grandmamma's journal as 'dear Ernest' and 'darling George'. Dear Ernest was preserved by his cassock; darling Gorge's ships went to dangerous places, and a great deal of God's mercy was called for. The oldest son died of tuberculosis, having been sent to Australia as a last resort.

The puzzling thing about this true religious zeal was again its conformity. We listened to sermons on Faith, Hope and Charity, but Charity was evidently uncalled for in other religious aspects, and the word always held hints of the Poor Law. We were C. of E., and every Sunday we met families of my father's pupils going in the opposite direction, to the C. of S. The fathers doffed hats, the mothers barely bowed; after all, they had not been officially introduced. Each thought the other held mistaken beliefs: the Episcopalians were proper, the Presbyterians were 'genuine'.

> "Pisky, Pisky, say Amen,
> On your knees and up again;
> Presby, Presby, dinna bend,
> Say your prayers on your hinner end."

I can still remember the worry of going for the first time to a Presby service when staying with a school friend, and going on my knees to the floor, a long way as there was no hassock. The whole pew turned round as spectators to watch my struggle of getting up again in a confined space, but there was comfort in the peppermint passed along to help with the sermon, invariably lengthy and verbose.

The Presbyterians prayed from no book, so you did not know what to do at the right time. The Minister prayed 'from the bosom', and very impressive and unpredictable it was — you felt he might get personal at any moment and appeal to the Almighty for miserable sinners who had mistakenly used their knees.

MANNERS MAKYTH MAN

In the Church of England fold were many divisions. One of our clergymen was too High. He genuflected often, wore a fancy cope, lit too many candles and even threatened incense, and liked to be called Father. A few score of the congregation left. The next one was too Low, and said what he thought, acted plainly, and was not deferential enough at the church door as his parishioners departed. The congregation, largely female, all seemd to like one very good-looking dramaturge with a sure and magnificent bass, but something about him curdled my infant bosom. Later he left, became an actor, and successfully coveted another's wife. These experiences crystallised into encouraging reasoned choice.

In all the Protestant folds, Sunday was sacrosanct. No activities occurred apart from the afternoon walk, hatted, coated, shod and gloved, and with a clean hanky. Reading had to be Biblical or moral literature; we had to learn the Sunday Collect and repeat it to a parent, an extract that has always seemed totally meaningless out of context.

You 'played quietly by yourself', could draw but could not sew, and the neighbours sat by their windows to check on conformity. If anyone was seen in the garden, they were under a spyglass; if you had hung out your washing, you would be ostracised completely, even if you had a leaky baby.

First school proper was a dame school, kept by two splendid dames. One was a very loving woman, and the other had a keen intellectual brain. In an atmosphere of kindness, we were led, not pushed. At five, learning about the many mansions in St John's Gospel, or about someone always sitting there in De la Mare's little green orchard, you felt safe, and knew where you were going on the whole. At eight, at the end of term I was given the recitation

> "Oh fat white woman whom nobody loves,
> Why do you walk through the fields in gloves,
> Missing so much and so much? "

and knew exactly what it meant.

Faithful Nannie, still with us, used to push a bicycle up the long cobbled hill to fetch me home, and I used to bump down behind her on an unpadded metal carrier. Occasionally, someone's father with one of the early Trojan cars, solid tyres on wooden wheels, with a fat dickey seat behind, allowed us to hang on to the folded hood with our stomachs over the bulging back and our legs flying wildly, whooping and screaming down the heaving hill. If my father had known, he would have exploded. The keelie gangs at that time used to rush after the milk and coal carts, and hang on the back, but of course we were never allowed to, just as those were children we were never allowed to play with. Part of the reason was head lice. I remember Mother once found them on me, and I was combed out with a nit comb, drenched with paraffin, and sent to school with a note, instructed to tell my friends that I had a headache, the one and only active untruth ever detected in one I loved. Not surprisingly, I was sent home again and had a week there reading what I chose. The free libraries were producing books suitable for the young that weren't holy, and it was a feast. Children's books of the period were written for improvement, and who *likes* to be improved? Blood, thunder, baddies and goodies are much cleverer at improvement of the young.

Unfortunately, my older sisters had been at a High School, and it was made clear that a fourth could go at reduced fees, so the move occurred at ten. Everyone there seemed to be settled with their own friends, and new girls were equated with black sheep. Again conformity was all, and I stepped off on the wrong foot when in Latin we were asked to say "Weni, widi, wici," and I refused, saying that *my* father taught *boys* and *they* said "Veni, vidi, vici". Refusing to bow the knee, I was sent to Coventry, and it served me right, but it was long drawn out and painful.

School was a well-built establishment on an airy hill with a lovely view, but at that time it did not encourage you to gaze beyond textbook bounds, and argument was disallowed. As argument was rather a passion with Scottish gentlemen, perhaps this was character training for preserving marriages, but it was discouraging. I shall always be grateful to some of the staff who opened wide doors in English, produced lovely songs for the choir to sing, and gave us unlimited materials to paint and draw with; also an unconventional biologist who took us paddling in the Water of Leith to find our first microscope specimens, but otherwise school lit no torches. Reports always said you did not apply yourself, but never found out what you were able to apply yourself to. Kurt Hahn was unheard of then. Instead of becoming a citizen of the world, to be a citizeness of Edinburgh appeared to be the highest aspiration, and, with luck, to marry a citizen of good reputation and schooling. Hockey and lacrosse were commendable, individual action wasn't. The only act of daring I remember was when a real Earl's daughter ran along the rim of the gallery in the hall, amid our reluctant gasps.

To begin with, there was a splendid headmistress with an eagle's nose, a piercing blue eye, and hair put up into a wispy grey tammy. She knew adventure, wore thick woolly stockings, and always showed her petticoat at prayers. But she left, alas, and was succeeded by an intellectual who used sarcasm on schoolgirls, leaving them bolshy and bewildered.

We were told to Have a Hobby. At one end of term meeting a very old and shaky school-founder told us that she and her sister had shared a holiday hobby. This had consisted of cleaning their canary cages. When our hobbies were displayed, a Highly Commended was a cake of soap made of lots of other bits of soap. I tried to follow this example in the later war when soap was hard to come by, but it was a time-consuming and slippery business. Most of the hobbies were pressed flowers or water colour sketches of "Where I went for my holidays", and the exhibition eventually petered out. Nowadays the school outlook is infinitely wider.

Riding to school uphill on a bike was a breathless rush. One of the hazards was keeping the tops of your black stockings concealed by your knicker elastic; if you had gaps, they were known as 'smiles'. The Academy boys came rushing down the hill and checked up on them. Rich girls had stockings nearly reaching their behinds, but our cheaper ones were never long enough.

Years later, when our younger daughter had to wait for dilatory buses to get to school, wearing the regulation short white socks on purple marbled limbs in an Edinburgh winter, she was refused permission to cover herself up with black stockings to keep her warm for the journey. In 1957, they were considered 'fast', whereas in 1927 they had been strictly utilitarian, and in 1917 the prerogative of maids and hospital nurses, or, it was whispered, 'Cabaret girls'.

35

A PICTURE OF HEALTH

Some girls learned to cook at home — what rapture — but expeditions into the kitchen were at that time discouraged. In the richer homes where maids were still in the plural, they were usually called by their surnames, and the cook was always Mrs, out of respect, but they could not be your friends without subterfuge. We had a few prosperous great aunts in the south with large houses, and there, a great-niece being far more kindly looked on than a niece, I discovered the fascination that lay in the warren of passages and rooms off that lay behind the green baize door in the hall. In the passage with all the bells in it on curly springs, labelled Smoking-room or the 4th Bedroom, you waited until they had stopped their ugly jangle and then rushed along to see them quivering in their last throes before being answered. There was a clear hierarchy in the kitchen, but, unless there was a sadist knife-cleaner or a vixen cook, it seemed a far friendlier community than on the gentry's side of the door. Warm cakes, mixing bowls to lick, the red glow of the range with its winking brass rails for airing tea-towels, and the lovely smells, the shrieks of laughter and "Oh, isn't she a caution! " You got the comfort and praise you longed for.

Current social history has a lot to answer for in writing of these groups as down-trodden masses. If there were an 'accident', the girls were seen through their troubles, and their loyalties to each other and to their household were close. Nannies had a very different and difficult positon, sitting in the middle with divided loyalties. They had to preserve the status quo of the ladies and gentlemen and get on well with the staff so that they got some supper after the nursery meals were over for the day. Everyone had to mind their p's and q's though, as jobs depended on references, and you could not improve yourself without just cause. You had to learn your job, with no false pretences. Apprenticeship in other fields took seven years with a master artificer.

Back to school, however. Many of the gods we were given were false ones — alas natural kindness did not come top of the list, and yet it is endemic in the Scottish breast. In fact we were terrific snobs, a middle class, middle income, bourgeoisie. It is difficult to believe this now, after a second world war has given us so much more generalised experience.

MANNERS MAKYTH MAN

Scotland hotly defended its Scottishness — "Wha daur meddle wi' me?" — only if you had used the right thistly accent for expressing this sentiment, your friends would have turned away in shock. At one stage, when singing about building Jerusalem, we had to site it on Caledonia's pleasant hills. Although I was a native, my parents were English, and this made me an outsider, as foreign as a Pole or a Persian. It left me very ambivalent in the middle of a quarrel, and yet despite their early hate affair with England, the Scots, and Edinburgh in particular, had welcomed philosophers and foreigners with equal warmth, once they had been introduced. This must have been a man's world, where whisky can help and a man's a man for a' that. A woman had to be a lady, and if a lady was not 'all that she should be', she was out, in middle class circles. "Who *was* she?" was a frequent conversational opening. When you were dead, you were safe. "He *was* a fine man," they'd say, but it was better if you'd been born, lived and died locally. It gave you a recognisable background.

Later this atmosphere ceased to bristle around me at school, and we all had more work to do for the various scholastic stepping stones. Intellectual competion was not de rigueur, so you never knew where you stood there. Hockey goals were more important than alphas, and all the games players were fired with ambition. I lost any proficiency in games after wrenching a knee cartilage trying to defend a lacrosse goal, so my position was lowly, but it did give me a chance to know some of the staff in an enriching fashion, English, Art and Music being well endowed. We competed hard as a choir, and often won in competition as we had a wonderful musician to train us.

Some permanent friends were made. Many years on, they seem as subdued as I am in their memories of our Education. With them I went on endless bike rides, climbed every tree on Corstorphine Hill, emerging to airy, swaying views of the Pentlands, and out of their windows smoked the first cigarettes, daintily held between thumb and pinkie. With others, we created dramas, patiently watched by relations and maids.

Later still, friends with a grass tennis court and charming parents used to have lovely Saturday parties, tennis beyond the roses and then tea on the lawn, with delicious food and beautifully selected young men, in their first flush of student apprenticeship. Older than the giggling schoolboys whom we knew, they were conversational instead of tongue-tied.

THE ROPE BRIDGE

V   TIME OUT

Holidays carried haloes. During early years, we visited the South
West corner of England where there was a cluster of relations. The
father of these cousins had been a civil engineer in India, there was
some talk of a defaulting partner, and he had come home early to
Bristol. In their drawing-room was one of the glass-topped tables
beloved of the period, in which to display objects of vertu,
devotion, or whim whams. Each year, we rushed to this to gaze
yet again with a shiver at a group of verdigrised bangles that had
been cut from the stomach of a crocodile which had been preying
on women as they fetched water from a river.

In the garden was something better, a rope bridge. From one
very tall cedar, reached by a ladder, a rope spanned what seemed
to us an enormous distance, to a multi-branched apple tree. We
hauled a loop on a pulley back into the tree, whirled down into
space, and dropped on to the lawn, teeth chattering with excitement. There were two much older boy cousins who uttered blood-
curdling yells and pretended to lose their grip, and a thouhtful
girl a year older than I was. For six years she was a Friend, a True
Companion, met only once a year but rich in association. When
she was about thirteen, she died of some affliction of the heart;
Ada and Gerty had come home to the family hearth, and this
caused great grief and deprivation to me.

The older boys were always kind. The eldest, later very tall
and glamorous, was under R.A.F. instruction at Cranwell and

much sought after by the local beauties, whose photographs with swirling messages written across the bottom adorned his dressing-table on steps, in order of current preference. They were studio portraits, the eyelashes carefully drawn in by the photographer's brush. He became a gallant Wing Commander in the war, and achieved the top admin. post at Cranwell, but died suddenly of a burst peptic ulcer. His younger brother had a motor-bike and used to take me clinging happily on the pillion, round and round the Clifton Downs.

In a western dip of these lived a great aunt in a lovely house with two ponds in the garden, full of lilies and fauna, each with its individual smell. She was very fond of me, as my appearances were rare, and when I was seven and the silver tray was carried in at four o'clock in the afternoon, did me the honour of offering "Tea or coffee, my dear? " No one ever gave you a choice at that age: you were told what to take and that was the end of it. Going round the garden with her brought another luxury, a warmed nectarine picked from the wall. However, her gardener ticked her off for this. I think he had numbered them. She was Irish, and one of her sons had inherited a big house in that green country. Later, when the locals were demonstrating their dislike of the gentry, they came to burn it. The son was away and his wife came to the door. She said, "Do come in, but please do not wake the children: one of them has been very ill." On hearing this, the invaders begged her pardon and left.

Years later, I went on a nostalgic trip to re-find that house I had had first privileges in, but it had vanished. The name re-mained, covering a new estate of bijou residences and Bristol University hostels.

The other cousin families lived in Gloucestershire and Somerset, five girls and two boys in one, five boys and two girls in the other. The first household lived in a square house with an orchard and beehives. Our uncle was road engineer for the county, and for the first time, I rode often in a car with him while he checked on progress. From honey he made a product that was called bee-wine, which I have been unable to trace since. It must have been a kind of mead. It was considered very healthy for children, and in the red hot summer we drank it freely and slept incredibly soundly after it, so its content must have been potent. We had fierce droughts there and the water supply dried up, so we had to use a well. I can remember sitting in a round tin bath with the older girl cousins while a small jug of water was poured into the little basin made of our legs being pressed together. We washed in this, and I think the juniors had to do with the scant suds left after we got out.

Those were summers of lying in the orchard grass, chewing its juicy stems and conversing, or picking blackberries from the heavy hedges. These were made into enormous pies which followed huge hams from my uncle's own pigs at Sunday dinner.

The Somerset family were all younger than I was and of different habits. Their father was a parson, and every morning prayers were read before breakfast. You knelt with your nose buried in the plush back of a chair, the smell of which always revives when I enter old auction rooms.

The boys combed the countryside on bicycles and made competitive lists of the villages they had discovered, which they kept tacked to the wall of their private room over a stable. The girls were younger and rendered more domestic by their very efficient and beautiful mother. The boys ruled the roost in that household, and later when the five of them were working in five different countries overseas, my aunt employed Monday to Friday evenings in writing to each. These families are still a part of my life, sixty years later. Cousinship is a very satisfying relationship, near enough and yet far enough to produce friendship in a comfortable fashion.

Later in adolescence, further visits were made to one of my mother's brothers who had spent his youth ranching in Canada and come back to a tiny farmlet on the hills behind Monmouth, looking north into Wales. This seemed always serene. The house, a tangle of tiny rooms, the bath a tin tub by the kitchen fire, the bedroom candle-lit inside, but through the window the Monnow valley swimming in mist, and the sharp shape of the Sugar Loaf in the distance. A great cider press stood outside, a barn full of hay, the temperature of which had to be checked daily by pulling out an iron rod and feeling how hot the inner end was, and an aged horse called Tom. When I went there to stay, my uncle borrowed a neighbour's mare for me. As he was churchwarden, we rode round various farms on the hilly country-side, beginning on the steep lane outside which was paved with great slabs said to date from the Druids and used by Romans later. Owen Glendower had defended the local hill, and the whole area breathed of ancient times: wild Lent lilies in the fields, later in the year silent woods thick with foxgloves, and foxes barking in the night near-by.

When we rode to the farms, we were always entertained with home-made cider or mead, and on journeys home I was glad the mare knew the way. On one terrifying occasion, when riding up an almost vertical field, we heard a thunder of hooves and a great stallion chased us. My uncle realised it was after my mare and yelled to me to ride on, while he did his ranching manoeuvres with a reluctant Tom and detained the sex maniac. That ride produced some bad dreams.

The church, far down in the valley, was a tiny, ancient, beaut-iful building. On Palm Sunday and at Easter, it was a picture. As well as decorating the inside, the faithful covered all the graves with daffodils, primroses and moss, so that the old tomb-stones reared out of a trembling golden carpet. There was a group of bell-ringers who used to come to my uncle's for an annual supper of ham and cider, by various vehicles from rattling bicycles to horses. One bearded ancient whom I sat beside confided, "I allus wash my feet before the churchwarden's supper."

Father took a great delight in Summer Schools, and several times I went with him into lodgings in Oxford or Cambridge. While he sat through lectures, I pleased myself — it always seemed to be sunny, and there always seemed to be people we knew with time to spend punting or swimming along the then uncrowded rivers. In Cambridge, there was greater relaxation, as the College Backs are more isolated from the town, but in Oxford he liked to take me to every College he remembered, especially his own Keble for which he had rowed, and which I thought remarkably ugly. We went into Christ Church Cathedral and were shown round by a very old verger, snowy of head, rosy of cheek. He pointed out a place on the wall where, he insisted, the image of Lewis Carroll (whom he had known) appeared when it was damp. Did he know

Alice then? "Yes, and as for Dinah, I've scuttered her out of the Chapel many a time."

An older sister of my father's, the babe whom our grandmother had nursed escaping from the Indian Mutiny, was a sterling character. She escaped from home to become a nurse in the Boer War, and later kept home for my father until his marriage when he started a boarding-house for his schoolboys in the north. Thereafter, she looked after ageing parents and then housekept for 'darling George' when he retired as a naval captain. "They give you champagne tastes, and leave you with a beer income," he said of the Navy.

Having reached her seventies, she lived in the Clifton branch of the Girls' Friendly Society, until she found a top flat just in time for the German bombings on Bristol. She blenched at nothing. Darling George's accounts of naval engagements made my hair curl, but she calmly went on buttering her bread. In one battle, they had gone ashore to see to the wounded in some desert area and found a huge Moroccan soldier with all his guts lying out on the sand. They bundled them in again, tied him together with his cummerbund and took him to Medical H.Q. where he recovered, sand and all. She could have done the same thing with complete calm. At the height of one of the Bristol bombardments, she heard a midnight groaning outside her door. Opening it, she diagnosed a man with acute lumbago on the landing, so she heated up her flat iron and ironed his back under newspapers until he could get up again in time for the All Clear siren.

I stayed with her several times and in several places. Once in the country, where she had constructed an uneconomic box of a house with a lovely view at the back, an unlovely bungalow was being erected at the front and she was asked by her intending neighbours what they should call it. "Eyesore" she said, and to her immense glee noticed a sign in pokerwork on the gate some weeks later, announcing ISAW. Once I stayed at the Girls' Friendly, and had great difficulty obtaining a doorkey, as they then shut doors at 9.30 p.m. and I had been invited to a musical with darling George. Delightful ladies with hair of copper and brass knew him. They had names like Gladys and Vera, and a happy time was had by all.

A PICTURE OF HEALTH

During the twenties and thirties the world seemed full of aunts and uncles, all interested in the next generation, and each time I go to Bristol, some auntly ghost may pop round a corner. Either they are ready to take you to the Museum, which used to give us wonderful cream horns for tea, or secretively to show you a little booklet of paper slips, called Papiers Poudrés, to take the shine off your nose, and to tell you how they used to rub their cheeks with geranium petals when they were girls, to generate a becoming blush.

THE QUINTESSENCE

OF IBSENISM

VI   CHANGE OF VIEW

School still filled the years, and the richest interlude in all this
schooling was in 1927, the summer I was nearly sixteen. My father
was given a sabbatical term and, to his honour, he discovered that
it would be cheaper if we shared it than if I stayed at school as a
boarder. Being a classicist and historian, he had always yearned for
the European past, and with my mother, an older sister in the
throes of a 'nervous breakdown' (loving relations were then mistakenly regarded as the best environment for this condition) and
myself, we departed for Europe.

The first gimpse of Abroad was memorable. We embarked at
Southampton for St Malo and, on a May morning, sailed into
the harbour at the mouth of the Rance. Our first view was a row
of dockers' backsides. They were all sitting on their hunkers at
the rim of the breakwater admiring the sunrise and performing
their devoirs over the edge. I subsequently read that this is a
common habit of communities that like to combine business with
pleasure, and how sensible; but to a sixteen-year-old, how incredibly *French.* As we drove through the town, the windowsills
were spilling carnations of every colour, mostly rooted in holed
and rusting enamel chamberpots.

After some weeks in a Breton fishing village, we visited two
enchanting old ladies in Vevey, where my mother had had a
'finishing' year at eighteen. Her memories were largely of thinking
up interesting stories for the Roman Catholic young to embellish

45

their Friday confessionals, but her schoolmistresses welcomed her as the good, pretty and musical young lady they once knew fifty-five years earlier. A marvellous very foreign journey along the flashing green and angry Rhone towards the Italian border was not without excitement. The railway coach went on fire, and we were all decanted. The substitute train went by the wrong route, and we therefore arrived in early morning rather than the previous evening. Clear as a mirror is a picture of orchards, with swags of vines between the trees, the young corn springing between their trunks, the women washing their clothes in the brilliant green waters of the Arno, until at last Florence, that city of gold and honey, swam beside the window. We walked out that evening to the Piazza della Signoria, full of gilded light and deep shadow. Nursing mothers sat on the steps, babies nuzzling their olive breasts, the evening breath giving back the burning day's last energy, the statues of the Sabine Rape looming above them in the shadows, Michelangelo's David still glowing in the last of the evening light.

My sister and I had a bedroom with voluminous mosquito nets and a frescoed ceiling of pink cherubic bottoms. Next door was a young Italian doing his Baccalaureat. He was there because our landlady was a Scotswoman and his parents felt that this would keep him respectable. His name made a lovely euphonious chant: it was Il Conte Lorenzo Alfredo Maria Emo Capodilista. What a melody to intone, after Scottish monosyllables. Sixty years later, I found this name inscribed on the list of subscribers to Peggy Guggenheim's Gallery in Venice.

Sixteen is a perfect age to travel. One has the energy, the seeing eye, little background to prejudge with, and such an open book is one continuous ecstasy. The only jarring note was an English set who lived up in Fiesole: they seemed irritable and foreign. We were there in a violent thunderstorm, and a little drowning kitten invaded the house, only to be pushed out again into the storm, its tiny pink mouth soundlessly opening and shutting against the window, with the sudden summer hail beating down. I came back in disgrace for having been uncivil — yet in church the next day, they spoke of the fall of every sparrow being known. Contradictions everywhere.

46

CHANGE OF VIEW

We went with Mother to a Russian church which was deeply exciting. (Mass in the Duomo would have been depraved.) A gorgeously vestmented priest with a spade beard and a basso profundo intoned at an altar full of icons in rich Eastern colours. His predecessor must have been a much shorter man, as from mid-calf he wore what looked like old tennis trousers and tattered gym shoes. A choir of Gregorian chanting in deep velvet tones rose and fell, and the congregation came and went and talked to each other, and knelt and touched the floor with their foreheads, while their string bags of shopping lay beside them. In one was a gasping hen, with tied feet. We walked everywhere, in and out of dark churches and rowdy streets, and for the first time in life learned to make for the shady side of the street, as it was a torrid June. Botticelli's Primavera in the Uffizi seemed the loveliest girl we had ever seen, redolent of happiness, sunshine and flowers.

In July we went to the mountains. The head of the Florentine British Institute was the son of a former Italian singing master in Edinburgh, an earlier pupil of my father's. He had a large, charming wife, two little boys, and a country villa in the Appenines where we repaired as paying guests for a delectable month. The black cherries were ripe, and we climbed a tree and gorged, coming down half-drunk with rich thick juice of an ecclesiastical purple that stained everything. It was cleaned off the hands by lighting crude matches that let off a thick fog of sulphuretted hydrogen which bleached the skin to a dirty yellow and made us cough. While my father and sister sweated over Italian grammar, I vanished into the environs, where cottage doors were open to any stranger. Are they still, I wonder?

The villa had a resident couple with an enchanting tiny daughter called Raffaella. With eyes like the black cherries and a smile as sweet as their juice, she looked as if one of Raphael's painted virgins had produced her. She was an only child. Her mother pulled her blouse up from the waist and showed me her breasts. which looked as if they had been attacked by a maniac. She had had milk fever, and the cruellest of slashings had released the products of inflammation: only a tough constitution could have survived such toxaemia and manhandling. She explained quite simply that she couldn't feed another child, so wouldn't have one.

47

She took me one afternoon to another cottage where a woman was in labour, and the room was packed with her relatives and friends, rubbing and kneading and giving her drinks in the sweltering gloom, and uniting their explosions of breath every time she pushed. I didn't see the outcome until later, a tiny hydrocephalic baby hugged to her breast, but the dignity of the whole proceedings stays with me still. The Old Masters did not have to seek far for their models.

One cottage was a dream of straightforward living. Gabriele tended a flock of gentle, lop-eared sheep that munched the thin grass under the chestnut trees, while Luisa dealt with their products. Early in the morning I was welcomed in with joy and given a sheep to milk, a much simpler animal than a cow: you crouched behind pulling both milk sacs into a bucket while the patient beast flicked flies from its long ears. The milk was then put into a huge bowl made of a piece of chestnut trunk, and pushed near the fire to warm. Cream began to rise at once. Meanwhile, large flat stones were heating in the embers. A paste was made of chestnut flour and water, two chestnut leaves placed on a hot stone, a dollop of paste, two more leaves and another stone, until you had built a pile. Then a bowl of ricotta from yesterday's milk was fetched from the cool. When everything smelt right, the stones were laid aside and the pile of hot chestnut bannocks bearing their leafy imprints extracted. A lump of ricotta was put on one, it was rolled up, and there was a breakfast fit for the gods. This was what a home ought to be, and the light that shone on the manger of so many paintings in the Uffizi must have illuminated so many hearths like this one, with the gentle sheep lying chewing cud at the door, until their master moved them to fresh pasturage.

Mussolini's profile with jutting chin and tasselled cap was stencilled on all public walls, and while we were there, an Irishwoman in Rome unsuccessfully lobbed a bomb at him, so an edict went out to round up and investigate foreginers.About a week later a small posse of Carabinieri arrived in our village to investigate us. The interview was a bit incoherent, a mixture of Italian and Latin from my father, and dialect from them. Their commanding officer was not present. They explained that he had a girl in the next village and had taken the opportunity to go and visit her. It was a very hot day, and once they felt duty had been seen to be done, we all went down the hill to the albergo again and spent the rest of the day gossiping, quenching thirst and dancing in the yard to the proprietor's concertina. It played one tune, Valencia, but in hot weather this was enough, especially when you were squeezed against a rather smelly policeman's chest, and in the pauses the innkeeper's wife watered the dust with a bucket. The C.O. then appeared looking plump and pleased, and with many handshakes and professions of eternal friendship they departed.

On the way home from Italy, we stopped in Paris. My mother took a taxi and we drove to Montmartre as it was on a hill, presumed healthy, and was also cheap. At each hotel, she asked the driver, "Y-a-t'il des puces ici? " and by his reply judged the interior. After visiting about three, he showed resentment so we chose a hotel half way up the Rue Blanche and were thrilled to bits to see from our fifth floor back bedroom window the scarlet sails of the Moulin Rouge slowly revolving against the night sky. On the same floor was our first acquaintance with French urban plumbing: an unlit cupboard, with a yawning hole in the middle of a concrete saucer containing two foot-shaped islands. At the side stood a large jug, usually empty, and a pile of newspapers. We did not find fleas, but bed bugs in plenty, and it seemed a great game to catch them and squash them beside the mosquitoes on the wall. French wallpaper seemed to have an awful lot of rich petunia colour in it, a very economic measure, as squashed bugs blended well.

Each morning there was a pattering outside as a small flock of goats descended the hilly street and stood on the right doorsteps to be milked in situ. Whether or not this was our supply, I can't remember. In 1927, except for the odd taxi, there didn't seem to be much traffic, although what there was did like playing its horns. Mostly, it was old ladies in black with shopping baskets, carrying the ubiquitous long loaves, which smelt lovely. Everyone seemed to be a widow. There was always a great murmuration of them in the Sacrê Coeur up the hill.

The climb up on the Arc de Triomphe was wonderful. You

49

could discover the French love of arrangement. The Place de l'Etoile, spreading its fingers out, was so beautiful; the disorder of tangled traffic and non-stop hooting all around pointed up the calm of its conception. We went swimming in the Seine in a sort of bottomless square floating by one of the bridges, and to the Comedie Française where Sacha Guitry and Yvonne Printemps held us spellbound, although the French was too fast and too vivid for our comprehension. Mistinguette and her fabulous insured legs was dancing at the Moulin Rouge near our hotel, but this was not considered comme il faut. We visited Napoleon's tomb, wondering why they should commemorate a hero in a pink granite tureen; we went to Versailles and could well understand why the Misses Moberly and Jourdain had experienced their shared vision of Marie Antoinette's court relaxing at the Petit Trianon.

The highlight was an afternoon on the Left Bank. As we sat at a pavement café with iced lemonade, who should pass by in his beret and ash-speckled waistcoat but John Duncan, a dear artist friend from Edinburgh. He said he was going to visit a studio, picked us all up, and off we went to see Matisse. Of the Maitre I remember little, but his draughtsmanship hit you between the eyes. Lines went only where they ought, clear black on clear white. Coming home, we saw two toga-ed figures with bands on their brows, waiting to cross the street: Isadora and Raymond Duncan (not relations).

John Duncan had been, and continued to be, a marvellous support through a gloomy adolescence. On the way home from school, I'd prop my bicycle against his railings, and he would make tea and toast at a popping gas fire in his studio. He painted there in tempera, using extravagant yolks of eggs to mix his colours, and later designed in stained-glass, but always made time for me. He was full of sense and fun. I wrote to him once, sadly saying I hadn't been there as I had water on the knee. "Far better than water on the brain," he replied on a postcard.

In a house across his crescent I used to spend Saturday mornings sitting for David Foggie, a portrait painter, who kindly paid model's fees and liked his women large. Once at one of his exhibitions a plummy-voiced lady behind us remarked, "Why must he always paint the Proletariat?"

CHANGE OF VIEW

We came home to the marriage of my eldest sister that autumn. This was a climax to a period of stress that had lasted for some years. She had come from post-war Canada and obtained a Carnegie scholarship to study English and French at Edinburgh University. There were no educational grants in those days which were not earned in fierce competition, and the money gained was a loan, to be paid back from salary later. Marriage was put off until it could be afforded.

I was fifteen years her junior, and memory has holes. Her first University years she seemed to intone *Beowulf* all over the house, and in her last year she won the English medal in Professor Grierson's class. In the interval she had met a young medical student who at sixteen had lied his way into the last two years of war service, and then started studying. He was an amusing linguist with divers interests, and we always used to goggle at a book they carried about one holiday, called *The Quintessence of Ibsenism*. Being simple, I really believed this would be of interest to a courting couple, until one day I noticed them sitting close together and holding it upside down.

We were all very fond of him, but the parents discovered he was Roman Catholic, and shame entered the household. They could not bear to know, or think they knew, that they would be regarded as heretics, condemned to burn in hell. That there was so little interdenominational communication really shows up the period, not the people. Ernest, the Anglican monk, my father's brother, helped to clear the air. In Plaistow he founded the Society of Divine Compassion, as 'Father Andrew'. My sister taught in France, then in England, paid back Carnegie, joined the Roman Catholic Church with ten times the fervour of her young man, and they were married. The family atmosphere was bleak, but eventually forgiving.

At that time, hospital residencies were entirely unpaid, and money had to be earned, usually as an assistant general practitioner, in order to benefit from hospital training for six months and to pay one's mess bills there. The post-war graduates were a rowdy lot and needed their drink, and bills were subdivided by the number of residents, whether they drank whisky or water, so they often finished their spell with a load of debt. Further surgical

51

exams were highly expensive too, and, once failed, a spell of
further earnings was essential to make up the fees. By now my
sister and her fiancé were approaching thirty years old. A medical
practice was the answer, and in those days this had to be bought
too, on a sort of mortgage. An affordable one was found in
Suffolk, which was a deeply feudal area. The Big House with its
portico and its partridge-run estate owned most of the land, while
small farmers, small villages with huge and beautiful churches,
and as rustic a peasantry as one could then find, made the background, so they married into years of struggle.

They were excellently suited intellectually. The medical care of
the Big Houses was a head-hunt of the locally established doctors,
prepared to carry their gun or their cards at social gatherings. My
brother-in-law had no urge for this but did a sterling job on the
locals, who respected their doctor, realised he must be paid although he often wasn't, and generally came to him only in real
need. My sister was a marvellous cook, and they produced a son
and a daughter promptly. She taught them and some local children
during the first years to supplement their minute income.

Commons were very short, but spirits weren't. He went into
town with instructions to buy a pair of pyjamas to replace the
ragged products that were giving up on him, and came back with
a second-hand gramophone instead. Being greeted with my sister's
protest, he put on a record he had bought at the same time —
Richard Tauber singing 'You are my heart's delight' — and bowed
to his wife.

They often gave us hospitality for summer holidays, and it was
a happy house to share with them.

VII   A DIFFERENT DISCIPLINE

School eventually came to an end, and I was thankful. My last year had mainly been spent drawing. I had had architectural yearnings. However, an art career had collapsed for one sister, and this was held up as a Warning. There was very little positive help from school for an obviously unsatisfactory pupil, and the suggestions given were usually academic, towards some sort of an arts degree, or domestic, to a college that trained one for the Feeding of the Future Brute. I dabbled at the latter for a month or two, and then at last an opportunity for semi-independence appeared.

In 1930 at 18 I started orthopaedic nursing at the Wingfield Hospital on a hill above Oxford, one of the most rewarding chances possible. Most of the patients had tubercular bone lesions, osteomyelitis, an inflammation of the bone, or poliomyelitis and its crippling results, which were as chronic as it is possible to be. Our only medical defences were immobilisation, fresh air and sun, good feeding, and preserving the fighting interest of the patients. For them, this meant an interminable training in faith, hope and resignation; for the nurses, it was wonderful in that we were working with friends rather than subjects. Physical improvement took an unconscionable time, but mental improvement depended on what we could put into the relationship, and this brought rich rewards. We learned the real meaning of the slick phrase 'job satisfaction', in a way few are given. It was a period of great privilege and very hard physical work.

A PICTURE OF HEALTH

Discipline was very strict. We did not realise why, in our juvenile high spirits, as it never occurred to us how tough emotional restraints were for young men and women immobilised for indefinite periods on splints or in plaster casts, and probably it was just as well. The surgeon who had inspired the hospital, Gathorne Girdlestone, was a handsome, single-minded enthusiast with a sarcastic tongue, a sensitive ear, a brilliant talent and a warm heart. There was no room for self-pity: the patient must co-operate with the end in view, however many years ahead, of eventual independence, even with stiff joints. As the opportunity of understanding and befriending was omnipresent, it made a healthy atmosphere leavened by jokes and bubbling with cheerfulness. The fact that, unless it was pouring or snowing, the patients were nursed out of doors the whole time helped them immeasurably, although concrete was cruel to our feet.

Children's wards had school, morning and afternoon. Many of them lay on their backs tied to padded frames, doing their work by means of a head mirror. They took all this for granted, as there was always someone worse off, who had come in with untreated deformities. Older inmates developed their own interests — many, varied and unexpected. A public school boy knitted complex Fair Isle jerseys; university dons got involved in girlie mags or each other's sciences; an Oxford Blue had drawers full of baby-blue silk underwear. One old don of great distinction came in for a short-term operation, with a Gladstone bag full of papers. The nurse's notes on his admission announced him as 'Mr Bloggs, Old Souls' Cottage, Oxford'. For a hitherto untutored schoolgirl, it was a rich and complex tapestry, and we were kept firmly in our place by our seniors. If addressed by their names, they snorted, "Call me Nurse! " We did not try familiarity again.

For a hundred and twenty beds there was one house doctor, a Cambridge-qualified woman of high intelligence, who rightly took herself very seriously, and had a very neat hairdo of which she was proud. On ward rounds on blowy days, she used to drive the surgeon wild by holding her coiffure in place while notes flapped under her arm, until one day in desperation he grabbed a patient's net sponge-bag and firmly tied it on top and under her chin. After that she wore her own hair net. She did her job superbly, at least twelve hours a day, lived in a cottage in the grounds, and was a friend to all.

Apart from the two surgeons, and a group of invaluable ex-service men who acted as orderlies, it was a very female establishment, and developed some hot-house emotions on the home premises. We had a dishy chaplain who used to give services in the chapel, and he had his problems, being hotly competed for by the older staff. Most of us, young and irresponsible, had friends down the hill in one College or another, and our weekly half-day off was spent sharing their anchovy toast brought by a scout to their fireside, or going to the flicks followed by a half-crown dinner of three courses and a glass of wine at one of the many cooking dens off the High. One of my friends was strongly committed to the Brave New World, as were we all in theory, and edited a magazine called *Plan*. There were a myriad others, usually titled by a plangent monosyllable — *Stop, Go, Look*. Their contents were fairly similar, — a well ordered world governed by The People. In summer, of course, there was The River — vigorous paddling on the Thames or dreamy poling up the Cherwell, gramophones under every willow tree playing 'Tiptoe through the Tulips', 'Who Stole my Heart away?', 'Tea for Two'. The words of these are still engraved on my memory, while Wordsworth has flown. The repertory theatre, with Stanford and Thea Holme and their co-actors blessed us with free tickets which were a perpetual joy.

For our varying services we received £1.00 per month our first year, raised to £1.50 for our second, which carried the responsibilities of working in the operating theatre (concentrating from 8 a.m. till 3–4 p.m. and then clearing up for the next day, eating sandwiches when they could be snatched) and the plaster room, where we had to roll our own bandages with dusty lime, damp them, and slap them on within minutes before they set solid. Our normal working hours were 7.30 a.m. till 8.30 p.m. with three hours off which might contain lectures, and a half-day a week. One day off a month brought the pleasure of breakfast in bed from the maids, but the thunder of feet from 6.30 on woke us up anyway. Night duty went on for three months at a time, allowing two days and nights off a month.

Our hospital buildings were left over from World War I. They were sturdily built, but at night cockroaches rushed about, and night duty could prove unnerving. Visiting a friend, I found her sitting on the ward kitchen table, its legs in bowls of disinfectant with an open umbrella over her head. It was the insects she could not stand; she had befriended a mouse that came out to share her 'dinner' at one in the morning. It was a topsy turvy life, night duty, as we had porridge and eggs at 7.30 p.m., a snack halfway, and after a tempestuous early morning washing and screening of our patients and passing the night report on to the Ward Sister, for which we had to be neat, in starched cuffs, we wearily went off to eat stew and prunes at 8.30 a.m. The digestion of youth is fortunately ironclad.

When on night duty we were supposed to sleep from 1 to 7 p.m. but occasionally a collection of pillows made an imitation mound in a darkened room, and the checking Sister missed it. If found out, we received a heavy moral lecture from Matron, usually ending in threats from her, and tears from us as we were, not unnaturally, tired out. Being told it was the patients who would suffer, however, always brought us to heel.

The end of night duty held a marvellous celebration. It was midsummer, and a friend came down from London, from her nursing stint. We took a punt complete with covers, food and books, up the Cherwell and spent two days and nights on the river, swimming in solitude and sun, well above Marston Ferry. Pure delight was sliding into silky warm water in one's skin at three in the morning, the moon ironing the ripples, the arrow of a water vole, the sleepy croak of moorhens and duck excited by the summer night, and our blissful shrieks. That was Leisure.

Back on duty again, some of us would escape through our windows on moonlit nights and go up Shotover Hill, mackintoshes over pyjamas. We woke a slumbering and blasphemous tramp one night and dashed for cover, but those silver evenings on Mary Sadleir's field, where the fritillaries grew wild, sing sweet still. I wrote home to say that was where my ashes should be strewn, when worn out with labour.

We were in many ways a light-headed lot. Lectures were essentially factual: nursing details, bandaging expertise, orthopaedic minutiae. We had come straight out of school, were astonishingly innocent, and in many ways this proved protective. With no preliminary training, we had been put straight on the wards, so that the patients were our textbooks, and their treatment our experimental procedure. It says a great deal for the adaptability of human nature that they put up with so much, but they were fixed in their beds, and, fortunately, we were not yet fixed in our ideas.

This nursing had not the crushing responsibilities of instant decision-making that beset the average hospital bed — this held a long-term-living problem as much as a treatment one — but we could not sit back. The children, separated from home and parents except for weekend visiting, needed a lot of cherishing, and the men, tied up and frustrated, were often a major problem that took all our patience and understanding. The women were marvels of survival and imbued a respect that has never wavered since. Worried stiff about husbands and children, they managed to contain these worries and help each other. On Sunday nights, after the visitors had gone, the wards were sad places. The women sang hymns, the children were either extra rowdy or extra silent, the men extra randy. It was a relief to have a half-day on a Sunday. Otherwise you came off exhausted, dreading Monday.

We did learn to deal with different human levels. The patients in the private wards resented their condition and often took it out on us. The general wards accepted their situation with the philosophy with which they had done the boring jobs in life. The young men had it worst: they found it hard to accept a future. A young butcher was brought in with a T.B spine. He made much of himself by boasting of the number of his conquests, and his companions got very peeved by this. They were infinitely tactful, though, when a threatening father with his bulging daughter appeared on one visiting day. Three weeks later, the victim was wheeled off to the registrar's in a spinal chair, and stayed under the bedclothes for a long time afterwards.

One youth with osteomyelitis suddenly terrified me one evening when by chance I was on alone by shooting a temperature above 108 degrees. I took it on two thermometers, which agreed. He was semi-conscious and raving, tossing wildly, so I drenched him with cold sponges. It actually seemed to improve him: he seemed better than I did, my knees were trembling so in a frenzy of inadequacy. When the night staff came on, at least there was help, and eventually I tottered off to bed, totally deflated by adrenalin loss. We had been taught that this temperature was beyond survival. In this disease, violent fevers were not uncommon, and often accompanied by acute pain, as a bone abscess developed. We had no specific anti-infective treatments then. He seemed better next day. Two years later, I ran into Joe helping his father with his Fruit and Veg. in the Market. All credit, therefore, to human physiology. Today it rarely has a chance to prove such versatility: anti-biotics get in first.

I remember with sadness one adolescent girl who had a tubercular hip. Her father was a High Church vicar, who had succeeded so well in impressing upon her that this was the direct result of sin that she was deeply depressed. We all spent much time with her, to make her feel that she mattered, but she never seemed to improve as her activated conscience helped to keep her down. We all found it extremely difficult to remain polite to his reverence. A smug little sister and an upholstered mother seemed to back him up, and they all sat there in a row on visitors' days, considering their visits a generous act. Of such is the Kingdom of Heaven.

One day I was preparing plaster bandages with an orderly when a large car drove up with a ducal crest on its doors, and the chauffeur bade us attend his owner. Inside was a remarkable woman bearing a minute slavering King Charles spaniel, for which she demanded treatment. We called out a surgeon, who politely told her that we were not qualified veterinarians. This enraged her, as she said it was an orthopaedic case. The senior surgeon arrived at this point and examined the small creature, which proved to be spastic. Hoping that the aristocratic owner might help his hospital funds, always in need of expansion, he took in the arrival which was duly shaved and given a plaster cast in which it could be bandaged. With short shrift the lady departed, and that was the last we heard; certainly no thanks of any sort were received.

A rather rich young pair from Cambridge came over to have their cartilages corrected in rugby-playing knees. They manned a Lagonda and a Lancia between them, and took a group of us over to the Spread Eagle at Thame, then hosted by John Fothergill, in his velvet jacket and buckled shoes. He told me I reminded him of a former favourite chow bitch, a rather unanswerable opening, but took the sting away by getting my signature on his Tall Ladies wall, then occupied by the very aristocratic names Evelyn Waugh later wrote his letters to. He certainly gave us lovely food. Another interesting expedition was to a handsome house on Boar's Hill, owned by an eminent botanist. His wife Lillah McCarthy, who had made her name in many Shaw plays, gave us 'attitudes' round the pool, looking very statuesque in a sort of toga.

We drove down to one of the Thames islands where an uncle of the Lancia-owner was staying. He had hired a river boat to bring up as many of his former regiment and their wives as he could trace for a day on the river, with strawberries. The whole boatload debouched on this small flowery space and had a delectable Sunday.

Thanks to my father's friends, I had privileges of entrée into some of the Masters' Lodgings, and still remember the bliss of spinning down the hill on a bicycle after a long night's duty to a breakfast table full of sparkling silver, bacon and mushrooms, Oxford marmalade and courteous conversation. One wonderful old Master's widow who wore a Victorian cap on her hair and had married off six daughters used at seventy-plus to go and work at a babies' clinic, and bemoaned the fact that she had not been professionally trained. Her daughters had all married well — bishops, lawyers, medical specialists — but she had insisted that they did this in series. They were a very handsome group, and one wicked nephew of hers insisted that an Imperial Rajah, who was not limited by religion to one lady at a time and who was then an undergraduate at their College, had tried to acquire the whole lot at one go. Her only son became an eminent headmaster.

The city was still full of eccentrics. Gandhi, his disciple Miss Slade, and their goat were entertained at one College, and a fine procession they made. Led by the tiny gnome-man, with large glasses and a mass of wrinkles of experience, his dhoti round his legs and splayed sandalled feet, peering with infinite curiosity at the peculiarities he saw, Miss Slade ten paces behind, in white sari and contemplation, and a disciple leading the goat, they all walked down the High to the river, presumably in search of grazing among the fritillaries of Christ Church Meadow. There were still strange figures resembling Bunthorne in ruby watered-silk waistcoats, or groups of Hairy Hearties in their flapping Oxford bags of delicate violet blue and beige, Bulldogs in their bowlers, and Scholars in their flowing long gowns as opposed to the ragged strips of black worn by the Commoners. On academic occasions, solemn academics dressed with all the ardour of parrakeets. Their varied robes can rival the Orient when they emerge with dignity on a summer landscape, as they do still.

During the vacations, the place swarmed with tourists, who used to come and peer through windows in a remorseless manner. The family of the President of Magdalen evolved a riposte. They repaired to the leads of the roof with a covey of balloons filled with warm water. These were dropped beside the offending troops, invisibly bursting and showering their legs, which usually moved them away. They probably thought it was a College ghost.

Young men came up straight from school and would go into enormous sets of rooms. One I knew inherited three huge chambers in Queens College, with about half an acre of bookcase and long threadbare brocade curtains. We went to Drawda Hall and bought several yards of books, as much as we could carry in a couple of journeys, to make it look more scholastic— although once you read the titles you had doubts. In the centre of the chimney-piece was a mustard pot built to resemble a lavatory.

How kind they were, all those beautiful young men, ever eager to take a punt or offer a shoulder should work suddenly put us into mourning. They believed we were vocational (as we were, on that salary) and surrogate mothers (as we often had to be, if we were not Girl Friends).

At one stage diphtheria hit the hospital, fortunately only the staff. I was the sixth and last to go, and can still feel the trembling of Matron's hand as she pumped an enormous 10 cc. of antitoxin into one buttock, on which I could not lie for several feverish days. Then down to the Fever Hospital, a Dickensian den. To struggle for breath against what feels like an increasing fog of tough spiders' web in the throat is not a happy memory. There was one chamberpot for a ward of twelve persons; Sister gave me an introductory dose of senna and left, and I crawled on hands and knees to the facilities at the top of the ward and fainted there. The Matron wove her way in and out once or twice a week, well-alcoholised, and the staff were the sort only she could attract. The doctor apparently had the sense never to enter the wards at all; he merely discharged you after two of the bi-weekly throat swabs had proved you 'negative', a process that took six weeks in my case. In the interval, one of the faithful young men used to bring a punt up a backwater behind the hospital, near where we found a pile of Matron's old bottles, and I had some healthy outings on the river, never missed.

Following this episode, the mother of a patient who lived on a farm on the Wiltshire Downs invited me to convalesce. The son in hospital had developed a T.B. spine while up at University, and his mother, who believed all ills could be cured by fresh farm food and brown eggs, could not understand it. Lying on his bed in a plaster frame, his great torso nut-brown from summer sunshine, he looked like an advertisement for rude health, but he had to have about three years of back rest, at the age of twenty-one.

They gave me a marvellous welcome, mother and father, two more hefty sons and two daughters, and had slain a pig for the occasion. After a period of endless Fever Hospital slop, I did less than justice to their great kindness, but soon perked up. On returning to the hospital, I slipped and damaged the knee that had suffered at school, and they decided the cartilage must come out. It still did not work, and a second operation removed a handsome piece of pearly bone, called a 'joint-mouse', which I gave to one of our orderlies. Being a handyman, he made it into a tiepin for himself, worn on high days and holidays.

The knee still gave trouble, and they thought it was due to a septic focus somewhere, and suggested removing teeth and tonsils. My teeth I managed to retain, but they dug out the remains of the tonsils previously removed on the dining-room table in youth. This is not a pleasant operation to watch, and a friend who was assisting in the theatre fainted all over the table, causing more difficulty than they bargained for. After this, my leg was put in a large plaster spica in which I thumped about for some weeks, and then a caliper. After a few months, I was allowed back to nursing whole in limb, and much better informed about patient problems.

Our hospital was changing though. Our surgeon played a carefully arranged game of golf with Sir William Morris of Cowley fame, who, at the nineteenth hole, signed a cheque for him to start rebuilding an up-to-date hospital. The huts, the insect friends, the making-do slowly changed to bricks, mortar and effective plumbing.

The barracks we had slept in had their windows wide, winter and summer. We weren't going to risk tuberculosis. A fat central heating pipe which warmed the ceiling went through all our cubicles, leaving a space between plasterboard walls, and there vociferous sparrows nested on its tepid surface just above our bedheads, so that in spring we had to sleep under open umbrellas. We left these rooms and the dire shortage of bathrooms without a tear, but we did mourn leaving the spinal carriages — cane-sided coffins on wheels in which we pushed patients out and had an understanding with certain of the Oxford cinemas who let us in free when thus accompanied. The joy of these was that we slept outside in them in summer, a nightingale in a lilac tree as a lullaby. We used to talk half the night away, but such is the intensity of outdoor sleep, we never seemed to tire.

My final hospital nights were spent sleeping on the flat roof of our new hostel building and celebrating a twenty-first birthday on it in moonlight and mist with chosen cronies, hauling bottles of cider up on a rope and feeling deliriously wicked.

Then it was time to move on, from what was by then the Wingfield Morris Hospital, now known as the Nuffield Orthopaedic Centre.

Contemporaries for the most part either went on to London hospitals to qualify fully after three years of further training, or into what was then known as 'massage' (now physiotherapy), a two year course. There were not then all the mechanical aids we are now used to. As so many patients had poliomyelitis, violent stimulation was avoided and a lot of passive encouragement was given to the circulation and to the surviving nerve paths.

I wanted to try radiography, blithely thinking it to be like ordinary photography, and went up to London to be interviewed by one of the early radiologists. One of the pioneers, he was more of a spirit than a man, almost transparent, deeply passionate, deeply courteous, a wraith with stumps where several fingers had been lost in the early experimental days. Now, we would say he was a victim of radiation sickness, but that did not stop him. He told me that one had to work sheathed in lead, and that all the best textbooks were in German, following Roentgen's breakthrough, so it was essential to learn this language. When I had, he would take me for training.

It all sounded breathlessly exciting and dangerous, and I went home to wean my parents to this idea. As I had been semi-independent for two years, when one pound could perform miracles, it seemed a reasonable request.

VIII   BERLIN IN CABARET TIME

To help me learn German, somehow we found an exchange. A dull Berlin youth came to stay and started me in pedestrian German. Three months later, at the age of twenty-one, I set off for Berlin, for a Junker family on a large estate about ten miles from the city. It was a remarkably fine feudal set-up. The Baron, known as Onkel Börki, was a twinkly tiny man, with a large, buxom, bustling wife. They had three children, Marlene, a daughter of twelve, Werner, a spastic son of ten, and Achaz, about seven. They were high in the Almanach de Gotha ratings, and the Baronin's family had intermarried so often with the Baron's to keep the genes in a state of purity that they had deteriorated en route. 'My' family were full of vigour and intelligence, but of the flood of cousins and in-laws that came and went, there were some very poor specimens, deaf or blind or undersized, or kept under permanent care, but all had a welcome in that sprawling Schloss.

After dinner in the evenings, about thirty pairs of hands would join in a frenzied free-for-all at 'Rasende Teufel' (Racing Demon) on the billiard table, with an uproar of shrieks and groans and yells, and sometimes bloodied knuckles.

The servants were part of the central family — in fact Onkel Börki's description of a gentleman was one who addressed his brother and his servant with the same courtesy, a philosophy I have never heard bettered. Robert, the old butler with trembling hands, was infinitely kind to an inarticulate young foreigner, and showed me how to cut roses out of butter and arrange pastry butterflies on mounds of spinach. Brigitte, the table-maid, with her smooth blond hair, wreathed plaits and Madonna's face, was saving up to be a nun.

"Warum? "

"Weil der liebe Gott so gut ist."

Alfred looked after the hens, and I worked with him sometimes, driving to market to sell the produce. I remember the hilarity when I came back and got the verbs muddled, proudly announcing that I had been sold there. Every fortnight a pig was killed, so I used to go to Berlin on that day, returning to find frenzied activity of pickling barrels, Wurst skins, jars of salt, and the smokehouse heating up with oak chips. All there was left to show of the pig was the tail, which the current kitten played with.

The alternate fortnight, the major household activity was in the laundry. Everyone had at least twenty of everything: chemises, nightgowns, voluminous drawers, and these were soused and steamed and thumped in a supreme chaos of gossip, then mangled, and dried in the lofts, then ironed in rows with huge flat-irons on which you spat to see if the heat was right.

In October there was a marvellous fortnight called the Kartoffelbuddl, which in Scotland was known as the Tattiehowking. There was a vast acreage of rich reddish chocolate soil of the flat lands, covered in potatoes. We all converged on this, and grubbed up the potatoes by hand into great baskets which were tipped into flat carts drawn by splendid horses, rather like Percherons. In the evening all the gathered haulms were set on fire and we roasted new-gathered potatoes in them, then slashed them open and put in a dollop of tart plum jam, 'Pflaumenmuss'. Then we came home under the pale young moon to a bath and dinner.

The house had a sort of cavaliere servente resident there, with a relationship of some sort with the Baronin. She was round and darling, he was emaciated and repulsive, and had given himself a 'von' which was quite unjustified. When I was in the bath one night, in a huge room where a huge stove roared to heat the water, he pushed his way in, and I had the great satisfaction of scoring a bull with a large and soaking sponge. It was pleasurable to see him arrive late at dinner in fresh clothes, looking like thunder.

There were tennis tournaments in Berlin to which we drove in a huge car, and several balls in Hotel Adlon, to which Onkel Börki, ever gallant, took me, and waltzed through three spare collars which he carried in a bag embroidered 'Kragen'. He barely reached my shoulder, so it was a hard day's night for him.

They kept certain saints' days, although the family were Lutherans. In church the ladies and gentlemen sat separately, and in black. On All Souls, October 31st, relations gathered from all the airts with enormous wreaths, and we processed to the family graveyard in the park, and then back for a service and a substantial supper. On All Saints, everyone had recovered and gossiped madly over their piles of food.

Days in Berlin on my own were a new experience and exploration. I used to visit Haus Vaterland, a huge department store with a real waterfall on one floor, and a whole series of little tables lit from below with red lights, each with its own telephone. I would buy a *Daily Mail* and a colossal cream bun, having a passing thought of home, but no nostalgia. But ignorance produced shocks. I wanted new stockings, went into a shop called Hosen and found they only sold trousers. And I came home thunderstruck after seeing a notice 'Zum Aborte'. Having been reared on Worse than Death information, I took some time to realise this meant 'To the Lavatory'.

Some of the shop-windows were unique, totally different from the well-known scene of Princes Street, or Oxford Street for that matter. There seemed to be a vast number of Friseur which I got right — red and white striped poles stuck out above their doors. There were also many purveying Baumkuchen. These windows held a shining metal spindle rotating in heat over a gutter. Batter was poured over this, which sealed on it, to be followed by further libations. When a certain number of layers had accrued, the spindle was removed, and the beautiful fluted cylinder of cake was sliced laterally and sold in discs, ready to be taken home for tea or munched along the street. In section, they looked like elegant tree trunks and tasted delectable. In Unter den Linden a shop sold engineering equipment and had a most fascinating display. A series of spaced ball bearings ran in and out of tunnels, up gradients and leapt into space and landed in gutters, a perpetual mobile run entirely on gravity and inertia. There were also innumerable coffee shops with pavement tables from which to watch the world.

At one stage, I could really prove useful. Schwester Lisa, the spastic son's attendant, came in great distress to say that her mother was dying. She went home and I acted for her with Werner, practising speech and exercises alternately. His spastic laughter over my German was a tonic for both of us; he would lurch over, and we would land in an undignified heap, giggling.

Winter came, and rides in a sledge behind two robust horses. We were wrapped up in fur rugs, and there was a great fuss if the horses forgot themselves, a yard in front of our faces.

When my time with these kind people was up, and the language learning by no means completed, I went into the big city and searched for digs from which to register at the foreigners' wing in the University. In the cheapest area down by the river I found a bedroom with a great white stove in it, lighted late in the evening. Too late was the discovery that it was one of the few blocks in the area with only single glazing in the windows, which during that arctic winter was a severe lesson. The night of my arrival, the landlady's other lodger hit her with a saucepan, and she asked me to watch him while she fetched the police. She came back later having thought better of it, and fortunately he had remained passive. In the room next door slept two bakers during the day, replaced by two railway porters during the night. No problem to warm their beds up, but mine was always icy, and the Decke provided, a sort of feather overcover, was thin and narrow. I had to lie rigid to avoid icy draughts, feeling like a figure on a mediaeval tomb.

That was the winter of 1932. Berlin lay under thick snow, constantly recurring, through which wandered an army of unemployed, thinly clad, red with cold, raddled by hunger. One took off his jacket in the street one day, threw it over a pigeon, plucked a few feathers after screwing its neck, and started on it raw. The streets and courtyards were full of women singing in faint voices for pfennigs. Politics were a tangle, the Reichstag was stifled with about twenty independent parties, but the great national dread was the growth of Communism. Every man without a job was regarded as an incipient Communist, and received little help. As an antidote to this, those yearning for safety flocked to the National Socialist banner. Disciplined hordes of well-fed khaki-upholstered youth marched through the town singing with their flags, followed by their leaders. They looked healthy, knew what they wanted, and were going somewhere, unlike the poor wraiths that crept along the pavement alone or in forlorn groups. Scuffles broke out all over the place which we, God help us, regarded as inevitable, like school rugby matches. One can live in such a state of blindness when one's personal life is on an even keel. Damage and death seemed incidental.

The Foreigners' wing of the University was a real international bedlam, but we were well taught German grammar, literature and script, and had to work really hard, eight to midday every day. Then we repaired to one of the restaurants Aschinger, where for 60 pfennigs we got an enormous bowl of soup with pigs' knuckles in it, and free bread, as much as we could eat. This generosity was later abandoned as people went in for the free bread alone. The University canteen gave a vast and delicious omelette for one mark, but that was a special treat. Twelve RM went to the pound in those days.

In the afternoon I worked alone, or went to my tutor, or talked with some of the many nationalities I met who, needless to say, had no inhibitions about practising their English. I was in no position to retaliate in Polish, Turkish or Czech. Politics have always seemed to be an opening gambit in Europe as the weather is in Britain, and many of these young people were well aware of what was coming, whereas I, and a few fellow Britons, were so deeply curious about life in general that we looked no further and soaked up the immediate moment without question. Political tangles had no meaning.

The government at the time showed an amazing sensitivity in one way. Unemployment was heavy, shops and offices everywhere to let, the outlook totally obcure, but, rather than add to the desperation, they kept the opera, the theatres, the concerts subsidised, and you could get a paper ticket off the grocer's counter which, with a student's card, admitted you for a pittance or free. The Circus Busch was near my digs, and some marvellous free evenings were spent there. There were four musical clowns wearing wreaths of bells round wrists, elbows, legs, necks and on their hats, and they had mock fights during which the strains of well-known melodies emerged. The trapeze artists swooped higher than I have ever seen them since, and the horses gave superb dressage performances; there was no hunger in the stables.

The Music Conservatorium was under the aegis of other Busches, the brothers Wilhelm and Adolf, and they gave frequent concerts. Wilhelm would have his back to the auditorium as he sat at the piano, conducting with a free hand while the orchestra followed his lead. One night, two British performers were billed, Harriet Cohen at the piano, Lionel Tertis with his viola. The British Embassy appeared in force, dinner-jacketed, the ladies in white gloves, and an elegant little patter of applause broke out as the artists appeared. The German audience at the back in the cheap seats where I was were silent. The performance produced enchantment as only these two performers could generate it. At the end the Embassy party patted its hands together again, but the Germans roared their applause — they had come out of curiosity and had been inspired. It was a splendid demonstration of heart over head, a Jewish pianist and an English violist. They had little expectation from British music then, and responded with all their intelligence.

Afterwards, with an English friend, I went to have a drink Unter den Linden. Two fire engines screamed by, and we languidly discussed what might be burning. In the morning we knew. It was the Reichstag, and the Dutchman van der Lubbe had been arrested as an incendiary. Already the next day the prophets said that it was a put-up job, and that the Nazis had started it, as was later proved. But in our ears still rang the magnificent ovation given by the Germans to a piano-playing Jewess and her inspired and gentle colleague.

There was a large dance-hall called the Restaurant Clou, and a group of us went often to spend the evening there, where we could dance for little more than the price of a cup of coffee, taking strenuous exercise into the small hours. Coming home was a bit hazardous, though, and I usually got trailed. Being built large, I found for some reason that my trailers were usually small, fat and importunate, but the tenement door made a fine slam after I had got it open, and I was slick with the key. Berlin air has a peculiar kind of invigoration of its own: at no other time has so little sleep been necessary, and the cold stimulated us to incessant exercise and hard mental work. Transport was cheap, but we walked everywhere.

The city had large blocks of flats, but no columns of doorbells that you could pull to notify arrival at the main door, which was locked. The more expensive had talking-grills, connected with the flat of your choice, but otherwise you shouted loudly from the street. If you were lucky, someone heard you and threw down a wrapped key which you groped for, but everyone knew who had callers that evening.

Inside, the flat would consist of a series of formal, almost identical rooms, each with a severe sofa, usually antimacassared. Only later did I realise that these still sitting-rooms became bedrooms by night. Entertainment was not done among friends slumped on their spines in easy-chairs. The group sat upright round a table with a plush cloth, a lace cloth, and a vase of flowers, bowing to each other in turn as they drank wine. As a visitor, you always brought a bunch of flowers with you. Coffee was expensive, tea quite prohibitive, so the tea-leaves were used and re-used several times. If milk was added you could taste nothing, so milkless tea has remained a habit into easier times.

The bookshops were loaded with English books, the leading sales apparently being Oscar Wilde and George Bernard Shaw; at least one play of each was performed all the time I was there. Homosexuality was known as 'the English disease', yet it was quite open in Germany. I had once had a bewildering passage with an undergraduate in Oxford with whom there had been an interesting conversation on the river, and we went back to his rooms to continue it. He produced a lamp with a glass chimney in it, then opened a bottle of claret and went through an elaborate ceremony of warming the glasses over it before decanting the wine, and we talked a little more. Then he announced out of the blue, "To tell the truth, my girl, I'm a bloody nancy." I hadn't the faintest idea of what he was talking about, and none of my friends knew either.

70

BERLIN IN CABARET TIME

In Berlin, I really learned about Christmas. In Scotland, it was an enclosed family occasion: in Germany it was all over the streets, the sharp smell of the spruce trees standing everywhere with real snow on their branches glittering under the lamps, real candles, brilliant shops, their door emitting wonderful smells. Because I was alone at this time, it was paradisal and poignant. Street singers sang 'Stille Nacht, heilige Nacht' at every corner. Most of them were thin and desperate.

I spent a spectator's Christmas, the loneliest of my life until then, but I did go back to the Schloss for the tenants' party, a magnificent affair with a fifty-foot tree in the hall. The house was crammed with relations, and they made me an honorary cousin. Although very lonely, it was almost better being a spectator rather than a participant, as against all the wealth of the glittering Kurfürstendamm and the Linden gloomed the awful poverty — stuffed pike indoors, raw pigeon outside. It was a relief when the University started up again.

However, Berlin was explanatory, and Christopher Isherwood and that brilliantly accurate film *Cabaret* have illustrated it well. There were specific cafés where you went as a drinker, a voyeur, or a participant, and I innocently attended some of these until the pfennig dropped. It took a long time, as they were all so interesting, but what finished me was one I was taken to by an American girl, called 'Der Liebe Frauengarten', where large butch women, some with monocles, danced round with clinging little floosies. For the first time I really wanted to run away. It is interesting to discover how restful communication with male homosexuals can be, but how uneasy with those of one's own sex. It is too difficult to penetrate, one fudges the issue with gut sensation that too quickly becomes prejudice, but in Berlin one got used to gentlemen, sometimes in drag, and with painted fingernails. In the meantime the Nazi noose was tightening, and several contemporaries in the Foreigners' wing took poison, jumped out of windows, or simply disappeared. Three whom I knew committed suicide.

I had joined a local choir and had an expansive time singing for pleasure with a very temperamental and deeply musical conductor who threw chairs when enraged with us. The other members came from every level, rather like a Welsh choir, and we opened our mouths and sang with releasing joy.

I was asked to teach free English to some of the unemployed, and found a group of about twenty highly intelligent men, many of them sacked from their businesses, some beginners, others articulate, so we really had conversational practice. When I had to leave at very short notice, these incredible people with no money gave me an illustrated book on Berlin, inscribed with all their names, which I still cherish. I also had to help two small boys whose father had gone to America. He was Georg Gross, the cartoonist. The granny with whom they remained wanted them to be grounded in the strange language they were going to meet. This gave me just enough money to get by on, as living was cheap. My parents were beginning to get very bothered by what they read in the newspapers back home, and used to send bundles of *The Scotsman* to prove it, but these proved most useful for twisting into tight knots and damping, when they would sustain a sulky heat from the vast white stove in my room, which was provided with three fire blocks only nightly. Washing was done in a china basin with about a pint of warm water dumped by the landlady; the loo was a dark and noisome cupboard.

One very interesting contact was a photographer on the *Berliner Illustrierte*, a magazine beautifully illustrated. He was on a commission to portray the rundown areas of the city, the huddles of unemployed, the broken windows, the countless notices 'Zu Vermieten'. I tramped round with him a lot, and started to develop a more seeing eye. The other side of the coin was illustrated by Goebbels and von Papen coming to shout politics at us in the University, and, an indelible memory, old Hindenburg like a rock of granite looking down from some ministry window while the khaki hordes sang and stamped by, flags flying. It was only then, blind and deaf as I was, that I realised they were after the Jews, and yellow stars started to appear, their owners shrinking by the wall.

This was all suddenly cut short by news from home. Our mother had fallen and broken her arm badly, I was the 'nurse', and ordered to come and work at it, so at twenty-four hours notice the photographer waved me off from Hamburg, where I had a dash round to look at the Chiligebäude, an architectural novelty we had all been pressed to see, and then walked up the gang-plank of a boat bound for Leith. Seeing a round-bellied sailor, I said,

"Wo ist mein Gepäck? "

"What like is it?" he replied, and I knew I was going home.

It was a rough trip, and the captain and I breakfasted and dined in solitude. Our one conversation was short.

"Can ye swim? " he asked.

"Yes," said I.

"It'll dae ye nae guid," said he. It was quite good to stand on cement again.

I went to declare my blazingly new German camera, purchased with birthday money. The docks taxi-driver asked me what had held me up, and I told him.

"Wumman, could ye no' tell I had a poaket? " he said, displaying a small sack stitched in his coat lining. I drove home feeling rigid with virtue.

IX   THE OPENING TUNNEL

Home in a chilly March seemed desperately flat. At least there was work to do at first, for if anyone was ill my father used to tramp the house and kick things, and the last sister at home used to become a hermit. Only Mother's company and Nannie's fried bread sessions, very bad for one's shape, seemed positive. The X-ray training had been postponed so that my German could be improved, but when I wrote about it they huffily replied that I had missed the intake. Our own doctor, for which I shall always honour him, noticed my despair, and we had a discussion in the front hall, so that it didn't look like a health matter to Father. He suggested that after enjoying such a particular kind of nursing, why not try medicine? It was a thunderclap, that anyone should think me intelligent enough to contemplate a profession on such a pedestal. "Of course," said he, "you will need sciences."

My father came out of this with great credit. He had retired by now, and busied himself in various friendship societies, befriending everybody but the Germans. He was so relieved that they were left behind that he undertook the weight of fees for an indefinite period, and for the next year I crammed physics, chemistry and biology into a head that had spent a year smelling the excitement of not knowing what each day would bring. It was a grinding year, but we had a splendid electrical Scot with a shock of red hair to teach us, who was as temperamental as the Berlin choirmaster had been, and he shamed me into some sort of discipline. The other students to be crammed were a stodgy lot, and seemed utterly juvenile after the mixed crowd I had spent four happy months with. The one outside exercise was joining another choir under the organmaster of St Mary's Cathedral, where we rehearsed. It is a joyous place to sing in: your voice leaves you for the choir roof and the acoustics are fine.

Possibly because the age of twenty-three looked steadier, the University let me in on a summer term, the third for the first medical year, full of fresh subjects. At 8 in the morning we assembled beside the Botanic Garden and learned basic botany and its relation to medicine, a sort of Culpepper foundation, accompanied by endless illustrations of potatoes, liverwort, and the life cycle of the fern. These were more home ground, and with a great puff to morale I was able to show my papa a prize earned as proof of industry. The pleasure of this class was that I could go home to breakfast after it, as classes were only five minutes away.

The anatomy room filled the rest of the time. We had lectures which had to be taken down verbatim, or at least we thought so. I then got my first taste of dissection, which was an eye-opener.

A large room smelling strongly of formalin, which the lab boys tried to sell us for ten shillings a bottle, contained about six benches, each bearing a corpse. This oozed preservative, and looked as if it had been soaked in the malt that we used to take with cod liver oil in childhood. These rooms were female only for the female students in those days, which spared one embarrassment. At that period, gazing at even dead nudity was quite a step. The bodies concerned told their own story. They usually came from the poorhouse — sad, malnourished old men and women bearing distinctive marks of their trade. The tattoos of the sailors, or the ladies who were tactfully called self-employed, the great blistered ham hands of the labourers, the pitted blue coal marks of the miners: it needed a lot of nerve to start penetrating these silent mysteries. Our anatomy atlases looked like national flags. Arteries were bright red, veins were bright blue, and nerves were chrome yellow. When we tried to team this up with what looked like a khaki tangle of dead telephone cables, it needed a lot of concentration. We also had physiology, which was more rewarding. By the next summer, when I had a spare term, having entered early, I was allowed to demonstrate this to the fellow students who were just beginning, and get paid for it. It was a growing up period as a psychologist, as two husbands and wives on the staff were in the process of swapping, and we had to tread warily. One of the wives had such phenomenal halitosis that the thought that she was worth coveting was most surprising. At that time, we all held our teachers in enormous respect: their word was law, and they preserved an inviolable image. To discover that they had rather untidy emotions was quite a stumbling block, but stumbles provide depth into education. Physiology took on a deeper meaning.

The lecturer whom generations of students will remember with affection was E.B. Jamieson. 'Jimmy' was a cadaverous figure with a face engraved by time, memories, and decades of dealing with the silly young. He was a Shetlander, always wore a skull cap and a sealskin waistcoat, and lived in one of the men's hostels. Very occasionally, he would ask one of the young men in for silent communion with his gramophone, for which he had a large record collection, and give him an apple to eat. He knew his lectures by heart and intoned them with total accuracy year by year, opening up the body verbally, layer by layer. If one was lucky, one could get hold of printed notes made by the industrious of years before and flogged to others. The opening lecture for 5th January was entitled:

HAPPY – NEW – YEAR – HEAD – AND – NECK

and this phrase was faithfully repeated by him the first day of the January term until he retired.

The back premises of this department were highly interesting in 1934, as they were full of pieces of dissection being meticulously re-assembled. A Dr Ruxton of Lancaster, whose wife and nannie had 'disappeared', was protesting that the police were not being helpful in finding them. At the same time, various packets of human material were found on the banks of the River Annan above Moffat, and were sent up for re-assembly. Pioneer work was being done by Professor Brash on reconstituting feet that had been chopped down to disguise their bunions, and jaw bones that had had prominent teeth removed, and by infinite taking of pains and some methods invented on the spot, a tolerable re-assembly of these sad ladies was made, enough to convict Dr Ruxton, to prove that he had killed and cut them up, and ultimately to hang him. It gave a peculiar frisson to see a bit of Mrs Ruxton's re-assembled foot, made of her bones and gelatine, being fitted into her shoe.

An unexplained oddity mentioned in the vivid book written on this subject was the presence of a 'cyclops eye'. This was a strange, almost unidentifiable bit of tissue that had been found, for which defence and prosecution both offered explanation, but the answer was not in the book and pathological science was then more limited. I think the prosecution tried to prove it was one of Dr Ruxton's pathological specimens, while he insisted it was part of an abortion of his nannie. I later met an old man in Suffolk who had been shooting on the banks of the Annan the year after the scandal erupted. His ghillie, along with others who knew the river, had been asked to look out for grisly remains, and to hand them in. For this service they had apparently received a per caput bonus. The ghillie had been unsuccessful, and met a friend who had done rather well by these means. Going home with a grouch, he found that one of his pigs had farrowed, and one of her products was a malformed monster. He took a piece of this, wrapped it in a bit of damp newspaper, and handed it in to Moffat police-station, where it was added to the other trophies and he got his fee. He related this with pride, and many chuckles, to my old patient, who said that I was the first person he had ever met who was interested in the case . . . R.I.P. cyclops.

The next year, the real hard work began, all the sciences I had only crammed suddenly amplified and needed a lot of mental resources that weren't yet developed. Luckily I met someone who loved chemistry and teaching, and he pinned me down to doing real work, for which I can never be grateful enough. He has gone on doing this for the past fifty years, although in old age I am beginning to find the work a lot harder.

During the long summer vacations, I had gone back to the Oxford hospital several times to nurse again, which helped them over the holidays and gave me the feeling that modest earning was sweet. We had many desperate cases of polio and one year an electrifying Swedish woman arrived, a physiotherapist who had very positive ideas on what could be done to help them. Up till then, treatment was essentially passive until the fever was over, and then the crippled patient had to get on with it with luck rather than management. Fru Chris ran a clinic in Gothenburg, and in summer went to a coastal resort on the Kattegat, where she worked hard on a small group of patients, and where they could swim in that very salty sea. I wrote to her expressing a yearning to take part in this work, but saying there was no available cash, and she replied by return that if I would come and look after two sisters, one a bad polio case, the keep and the work was there.

The August of 1936 was spent in Båstad. Gothenburg was a gleaming place to arrive at on the Newcastle boat, islands like whales' backs with gay wooden houses and boats at the front doorstep, and then a journey along the glittering coast, stopping at spotless little stations, the station-masters in white ducks and blue peaked caps looking like admirals, against flower-beds full of many-coloured phlox. On arrival I was introduced to an aunt looking after Barbro, aged ten, the polio girl, who had badly affected legs, and her sister Lisa. About three hours later, the aunt left, leaving an empty larder and some housekeeping money. She even took the toilet roll away. They had no English but did not seem to mind that my Swedish was in a phrasebook, and with Barbro in a push-chair, we went to market and stocked up. First we went through a ceremony of locking the door with a most enormous key, which was then conveniently hung on a nail on the door-frame in case we lost it.

Up the road was a houseful of fellow Britons, all polio victims, all of whom had been in the Oxford hospital, and one of whom I had previously met there. They were a hilarious lot, and the usual joy to be with that the cheerful disabled bring with them. Having gone down to the bottom with a bang, there is nothing to do but bob up again. One boy had made history. At school in his last year he had had an acute attack which affected his respiratory muscles and had been kept alive by relays of staff doing artificial respiration until one of the new breathing machines had been flown from America on his father's insistence. The respiratory muscles returned to activity, but his legs were practically useless and his arms greatly weakened.

The drill was that all the patients congregated in the morning, and Fru Chris oversaw the exercise of each one, helped by an assistant. She was the most positive caring agent I have ever met. She gave them large books of handsome naked Greek statues, and pointed out all the muscles being used. She then showed the patients where they ought to be, and started them off willing the finest movements possible, like bending one joint of one finger. Once it was proved that the nerve track was intact, they could progress to a slightly coarser movement. Progress might be nil, or infinitesimal, but hope wasn't. In the afternoon everyone was piled into cars and taken to the beach, where we might have to drag them into the tideless sea, but where they all seemed to manage to get about with what limb was left. After that we would often go and watch international tennis, as a sort of mini-Wimbledon went on, at which the old King Gustav of Sweden, calling himself Mr G., used to play with a well-known partner of international repute. Pushing one of the patients through the crowd one day, I saw an obliging space which fitted a wheelchair, and went into it, only to discover it was the royal area. However, Mr G. smiled kindly and waved us on in a very understanding way. Not many people were so obliging, although they all recognised polio: in those days Scandinavia especially had awful epidemics of it, and there was much crippling. There were two memorable fellow countrymen, though, who always gave us a greeting. One was Alvar Lidell, the newsreader, and the other Raymond Massey, the actor. Others averted their eyes from a carload of cripples.

Coming home from this episode was an event of note. The schoolboy's father was an industrialist who made shoe polish. He said the most valuable testimonial in their office was from an Australian cobber. It said, "Your polish is no bloody good for my boots, but it has done my piles a treat. " This father brought an aeroplane over to fetch us home. We all drove to Malmö, got into a ten-seater which took off over Helsingör, so that we could peer down into Hamlet's castle, and then cruised low over the flat fields to Schipol in Holland. Air journeys then were slow, low, deliberate and fascinating: the plane needed fuel and we needed food. We were given a Dutch sandwich — a slab of delicious bread covered with overlapping slices of pink ham, looking as if they had been carved off the pink Dutchman, and topped by a colossal slice of Edam cheese. From there, we took off along the Dutch and Belgian beaches, looking down on rows of decorated little villas, and miles of sand covered in children and donkeys, many of which were being tried out by plump Belgian papas with their trousers rolled up and bowler hats on. At last, we branched over the Channel and eventually landed at Croydon, then England's airport. The aerodrome looked like a stage set from a Coward play. The concourse had sofas in it, and on these sat sirens, apparently waiting for the exhausted air crews. One only needed an orchestra to strike up to have a thé dansant. We delivered all our precious charges back to Oxford, where I found *The Well of Loneliness* (fiercely banned Tauchnitz edition) under the bed and read it, feeling very superior as I had seen All That in Berlin.

That year was notable. Sweden had been marvellous, but I was yearningly in love with my chemistry coach, who by that time was a co-student whom we called Jim. His Austrian father, a professor in Heidelberg, had married a remarkable Berlinerin. Reared in great luxury with an autocratic old father who ran a large weaving factory, she had wanted to go into his business, but early in the century rich young ladies had to await suitable gentlemen. She had always been fascinated by science, and managed to get herself coached in Greek and Latin on the quiet, to gain her University entrance. Grudgingly, her father financed her studies in Biology, and in 1908 she was the first woman graduate in Berlin to make the grade, and worked with Virchow. But she came of Jewish stock. The Nazi beliefs were simple: pure Aryan blood ensured virtue. The irony of the matter was that her five very good-looking blond athletic children were severally pointed out as being perfect Aryan specimens. Their parents, however, could read the weather, and had what must have been the ultimate agony — to send their children, two still in their teens, away from the heritage which they dearly loved, and in which the professor, their father, had done a great deal of academic research.

Apart from his work in mediaeval history and civil law, he had been struck by the difficulties of the one-armed casualties in the First World War. He solved some of their problems by having each of his arms in turn immobilised and then testing how effectively to use the other. He was the first person to suggest elastic shoe-laces, but every other function was catered for in his book *Die Einarms-fibel,* which was still in use until effective false limbs were perfected.

In 1936, while I was in Sweden, this family managed to meet together as a group for the last time, in Yugoslavia. Jim had to avoid Germany and got there via Switzerland and Austria. After a year doing chemistry in Innsbruck, some of which had been spent helping suspected persons cross the frontier out of Austria (the Anschluss was to come later), he had come to Cambridge to work with an old friend of his father's, and was eventually accepted as a medical student in Edinburgh. Before leaving home, he had undone the lashings of his hockey stick, tennis racquet and press, gouged out the insides and packed them with his mother's jewelled inheritance which was thus smuggled through Customs and used to finance his student years, so he knew his way about. After these two 'holidays', our reunion was a very joyous one and we both embarked on the clinical years with zest. At last we saw what the grind was leading on to — an unconscious reflex to question and argue and buttress or refute every point. Of course, some found their way just through swotting, but, being about four years senior, we had approached these more mature levels from different routes.

We had sat through three years of lectures from very varied lecturers. Ministers of the Church are 'called' after a hearing, and similarly we can judge, if we bother, our future Member of Parliament. Yet universities continue to choose their academic staff on a limited interview and the fatness of the pile of papers which they have written, or edited, or shared with many other co-workers. These may be good to study, but when their author mumbles, has mannerisms or an accent which demands constant concentration in addition to his matter, this is a waste of everybody's time and talents. Respect from your pupils is essential if they are to learn from you, and this must be earned.

The knowledge that we were going to act, not only to sit, was invigorating.

NIGHT

IN THE DUCKPOND

X   THE WAY THROUGH

Suddenly, from being one-in-a-lab, you were one-in-a-ward, a
change of about five to one in identity. We were a very correct
lot. Right up until graduation we called the acquaintances of our
year Mr and Miss. To the present generation this is an hysterical
form of address, but it was oddly protective. You can get a lot
more edge, of friendship, into saying "Mr Merryweather" than
just "John", and it gives you a comforting armour against over-
familarity. Eventually you may reach "tutoyer" — and then
friendship is forever. The riches of university living are the friends
you make and meet and respect. They, and certain teachers, stay
with you always, long after what you were taught is lost, or out of
date, or reincarnated in fashion after decades have passed.

There was no time limit for taking exams in 1934, and there
was a corps of perpetual students. One notorious Chinese undergraduate was found at the Union bridge tables most of the day,
making enough money to pay his exam fees but rarely bothering
to work for them. Another youth, who looked like a dude, put
himself through his course by playing in a dance-band every night,
going home afterwards to do a couple of hours' work before the
morning classes. He smoothed his hair with glue, renewed fort-
nightly, and used to invite you to pat it. It felt like a hollow
shutter. After ten years he qualified at last. There were one or
two other eccentrics, not over-equipped mentally, who were
known over many years by many undergraduates. One rather

butch lady was so infuriated by my having passed an exam she rightly thought I was unfit to do, but which had defeated her, that she rushed at me with a very large shoe and kicked a vast hole in my only skirt, so I had to hobble home in a tram, pretending to cook up an appendicitis. Nannie added her patching skills to the fried bread that night.

Some of our mentors were nondescript, but many were memorable, men who having graduated at one university (too often Edinburgh, perhaps) went on to work in Leiden or Padua or Philadelphia. Only then could they start the arduous climb to consultancy and, unless they found a young lady with something behind her, could not marry until their forties. They then had to educate a family when they should have been easing up.

Our year must have had about twenty per cent overseas students. The city, with its Church and Medicine connections, held a large corner in missionaries, and to them Edinburgh was the lode star for their bright pupils. These products of the missions were exceptional in the way they settled in and worked and found their feet. Many didn't make it — they learned the book but the art of reasoning had not been acquired — and cold digs and lowered morale led, not too rarely, to infections. Several died of tuberculosis which they met for the first time, and these always seemed to be the brighter ones.

I don't think they were too lonely: many had gregarious backgrounds and the university was rich in society, and societies. There were far fewer hostels, but a host of landladies, many of whom exercised the most motherly and tactful interest in those they cared for, and also exercised basic disciplines over their manners and morals that could only do them good. Occasionally marriage to their daughters cemented the bond.

The University Unions were companionable places, and we forgave a lot of his statements if a man came from elsewhere. The foreigners, and some of the maturer students who came in from other professions, did an immeasurable favour to our locally-schooled group, who tended to be earnest and bap-faced, and timid of their teachers. The lovely loose-limbed walk of the West Indians, and their ready howls of laughter, still fill my vision. One Nigerian with thick eyelashes we swore he curled round pipe-cleaners every night, and a head covered with a crested mat of deep black fuzz, walked proudly in one day, stiff-necked and with a smile like a melon slice, wearing a two-inch helmet of snow he had acquired walking across the Meadows. The smile faltered a bit when it started to drip down his neck, but manna in the desert couldn't have given him greater pleasure.

We used to go into viva examinations in alphabetical order, and I always followed a huge and genial dark brown gentleman. Certain of our teachers were very limited in their views, and it was interesting to discover these when we found what mood they were in. If they didn't like women either, then I had a rough time. However, my predecessor graduated and returned to Trinidad, where he now holds a professorial chair. He always had a much better temper than many of our examiners.

Once we entered hospital wards, the world expanded to infinity. We knew why we were there, and were able to work actively with people, at last. Hospitals then were voluntary institutions, as were the medical staff who manned them.

Early morning lectures would explain diseases, signs, symptoms, and masquerading effects; then we went among the beds and saw their manifestations. We could choose our medical chief, who delegated some of the teaching to his clinical tutor. Good chiefs chose good tutors, so certain places were hotly competed for. We had to try and rush the queue for signing on, or sneak into the ward in the holidays, do some of its dirty work, and try to appear indispensable.

In the Thirties, the wards held thirty to forty uncurtained beds, and there would be one male and one female ward in the suite with a few tiny side wards for special cases of need. When we were full, which was most of the time, there were beds up the middle. The chief, the sub-chief and clinical tutor were supported by one houseman only, who thus carried an enormous burden. A few years later, he was given a clinical assistant as support. It must be remembered that those gentlemen (it was strictly a male hierarchy) had worked elsewhere before obtaining these jobs, so were not totally raw. Enough money had to be earned to support yourself for six months: you earned bed and board only. It was an honour to be chosen, and you paid for it in standing, but there were financial hardships.

The essential pillar of our ward and our real judge was the Sister, the captain of a crew under constant training. She controlled both wards, often lived in a bedroom and sitting-room off the main corridor, and hardly ever had off-duty, through sheer devotion or worry over new staff. One used her statutory half-day to bake home-made cakes for her patients as a change from their hospital tea, bread and marg., which then was a chunky brilliant yellow. The Sister, more than the Chief, set the tone of the ward, as her teaching and discipline controlled the nurses, who trembled in their shoes. The patients too held her in awe. She was the hostess with the mostest, they were her guests in the best wards, her tiresome kindergarten in others, but she was always the headmistress. Choosing a ward by the Sister, therefore, was just as educational as choosing it by the chief, and if you wanted a residency for yourself one day, she would speak up for you. They were excellent judges of character and industry, and the general treatment of their patients was superb.

We lived in a stable society then: when you had contributed to it, you stayed on and became part of the fabric. The nurses, too, stayed on in the ward for about three months, so that all faces became familiar — for the patients a tremendous reassurance.

We had a medical Chief of outstanding style and kindness. However, he had inherited a real battleaxe to run his wards. The sheets all had to be turned over the tops of the bed fourteen inches exactly, and splints or cradles against weight were considered untidy. When he bent over one old lady and asked her how she did, she raised a bleary eye, beamed at him and said, "Ech, you're a bonny man." Sister fussed along behind him and straightened her sheet. Her gaze hardened and through gritted teeth she muttered, "As for you, you're a right bizzum."

There was no question of changing the skipper. Sister had been there longest, so she was his cross for years. Yet she did her medical duty to her patients without a scintilla of doubt — only there was no personal love in it, but duty and discipline in starch.

At Christmas, the ward had a tremendous party, paid for by the Chief, and acted out by the staff and attached students. After a diplomatic battle with this Sister, who considered parties made for untidiness and slipped discipline, the Chief went round his beds, to see that no untoward problems affected his patients. The change had done them all good, and brightened the rigours.

He bent over yet another old lady, an unfolding of his tall elegance. "Have you enjoyed your party? " he enquired. A pause.

"Well, I've haird no complaints," was her reply. Praise indeed. This man had a wonderful turn of phrase. Years later, I was asked to give a paper to a meeting in Yorkshire and felt that I might judiciously quote him. On arrival, I was aghast to find that he was to speak before I did, so there had to be hectic substitutions which ruined the hoped for effect. At the dinner afterwards he was infinitely generous. We were blessed with our exemplars.

If you became well-established with the Chief, you were regarded as a Junior, and the ward could become your home of learning after hours. On the surgical side, Jim and I became embroiled in a superb set-up, good the whole way through. We became part of the supporting fabric and were given a lot of the routine work which normally as an undergraduate you had no opportunity of doing; by some miracle you were supposed to emerge into qualification well-equipped for taking off blood and other specimens, talking and listening to every variety of articulate and inarticulate patient, staying with the dying, and dealing with relations, in some ways the most difficult problem of the lot. We wore white coats, a stethoscope at the ready: this gave authority which fortunately we were well aware was skin-thin. We learned that what most people want is to be listened to, and authoritative ears of the staff are often busy and distracted.

In this ward, we had our introduction to the real humanity which was paramount. Our Chief, Sir David Wilkie, a nonpareil, was removing the thyroid gland from a young woman when she suddenly died. This was not a totally unusual event then, as sedatives were the only controlling drugs we had for this condition. Her husband, forewarned of the risk, was sitting outside. The Chief, with tears on his cheeks, went straight out and told him about it. Any lesser man would have left it to others.

An indication of his qualities was given at his speech at a congratulatory dinner in recognition of his Knighthood. He owed a great deal to the old nurse who had governed his youth, he said.

THE WAY THROUGH

Every Thursday night she had given him a hot bath, a dose of brimstone and treacle, and a beating with a hairbrush. He plucked up courage to ask her why. "There's others interested in your eddication," she said. "What I'm concairned wi' is your bowels and your character! " Q.E.D.

One of our contemporaries was in the Students' Ward at this time. She had a high fever and badly infected tonsillar glands, unyielding to treatment, which were to be lanced. At this period, Prontosil, the first of the chemotherapeutic drugs, reached this country from Germany, and she was given some as a last resort before surgery. The details were all written in German and this was translated for the Chief by my friend Jim. Such was the trust he extended to his workers. The results were spectacular. She became a remarkable ink-blue colour and produced alarming beetroot-coloured urine, but her glands subsided and improved. She became a pretty pink again as her blood chemistry became normal, and, despite a depressive aftermath, finished her studies.

The surgical team was completed by a gentle, calm, totally prepared Theatre Sister, whose understated expertise made every operation into a disciplined ballet. The surgeon extended his hand, and the right instrument was in it at the same instant, no words uttered. Concentration was so intense that it was the job of one of the Juniors quietly to utter a warning that the Castle gun was about to boom, at one o'clock. If this was omitted, the thread of tension would break and take time to tighten again, after Sister had leapt in shock. What an atmosphere to learn a craft in.

The anaesthetist was a dear old man who had been working so long that his reflexes appeared in the charge of his guardian angel, who was always on the qui vive, even when he left a smouldering cigarette beside the open ether bottle. Anaesthesia was always by inhalation, and a delicate hand was needed. Induction was well taught, and Edinburgh went on using chloroform long after the south was terrified of it. Our James Young Simpson was the first to use it, and we were the last to give it up. Nothing was better to calm an alcoholic, provided his liver was still an efficient organ for its detoxification. Unless the anaesthetist was expert, patients then often had a wretched, retching time regaining consciousness. One perforce stayed with them, but this was the least pleasurable

87

activity of the lot, both for those in the bed and those beside it.

Once a week we would have a Waiting Night, when it was our turn to receive casualties who needed a bed, transferred from the Out Patients' Department. This would involve being on duty from about 6 at night until 3 or 4 the following morning. One of the perks for the male students on call like this was that they were taken to the Residency for an ample, though often cold, dinner. Not the women, however; they were barred from such masculine enclaves. Our Ward Sister considered this unfair, and always had a splendid little meal ready for me, beside her sitting-room fire. I think she was unique in this. She, and all the staff of that ward, became life-long friends, and occasionally in subsequent years I would run into a memorable patient, who used to ask after everybody as if they were blood relations. It was a wonderful living and fighting atmosphere.

The work, of course, was prodigious. There were hardly any medical technicians then, and all the regular admission tests on blood, urine, pus and so on were done in a smelly little tiled cell at the end of the ward known as the Duckpond. As Juniors, we were often entrusted with this, and what was lost in accuracy was made up by enthusiasm. When the results were more than sheer routine, these were checked by the houseman. Every admission in those days was tested for syphilis, by the Wassermann reaction, done in the main laboratory.

One case stands framed, for sheer teamwork. Electric pylons had recently been erected in the Borders, and a desperate call to our second surgeon, J.J.M.Shaw, took him down to see a sixteen-year-old. He had climbed a pylon for a dare, his clothes wet with snow, had been electrocuted, and had fallen into a drift. But he still breathed. The diagnosis appeared hopeless owing to his injuries, and movement was dangerous, so he was thoroughly sedated in the local cottage hospital to ease his passing. A phone call two days later asked if we would receive him, and in wonder we did.

Both arms had been desiccated with electrical burns, and looked as if they had been pickled brown: half a buttock was burned away, and three toes of one foot. The sparks had darted through him with a macabre random. Ivan was a beautiful boy, with courage to match. Both arms needed amputation, an articulating shoulder left on one, and dressings applied elsewhere. These needed replacement every three days, and we wheeled his bed into the theatre, where he withstood great pain. He kept the whole ward going and was in for months, all of us revisiting him for a long time afterwards. Eventually the time came for him to have new limbs fitted, and he was discharged from our reluctant view.

Some years later his surgeon came in. He showed us a type-written letter, and a small feather cut out of stiff silver paper. The message read: "You were heard to say that if I lived, I should be a feather in your cap. Here is the feather. Thank you. Ivan."

This fine surgeon was one of the forerunners of the plastic remodellers and told us a tale of an early repair to a nose, whose end had been bitten off in a brawl. Paraffin wax was the remodelling base then, and his patient returned next year with a weirdly dependent proboscis.

"But what have you been doing? " he was asked.

"I'm a stoker, sir," he said.

Patients came to this surgeon from all over the country. A tiny four-year-old with his warm Jewish father came from Manchester with a gross, if one can thus call such a minute object — deformity of the penis. The rabbi at this circumcision had either met the bottle, or mislaid his glasses. The poor child could only dribble, and was shortly due to go to school, where all failures are inevitably under the microscope. Our surgeon, an enormous man with fingers like bananas, did a meticulous job of restoration, murmuring at the time, "There's a divinity that shapes our ends."

The triumph came when, at a crowded postgraduate lecture, in the presence of his beaming father, Harvey's tiny organ was aimed into a large glass winchester jar and, for the first time in his life directed a steady stream into it, with accompanying cheers from the audience.

At night-time hospitals generate their own particular atmosphere. Snores, tossings, groans, gasps, and the padding feet of the caring staff; subdued clinks, the night sister's torch at unexpected moments, a dimmed light, a rustle, the click of screens put around a bed. This was always an anxious sign — the need for a changed dressing, or a change for the worse. We would work away in our little duckpond cell with a bunsen burner flaring, a row of chemical bottles, a microscope and a light that was always difficult to fix directly; you felt like the stoker in a ship, with the powerful engine-room outside. When concentration threatened to split your skull, you went outside to see if there was a wakeful patient, and held a tiny, secret, whispered conversation, before returning to squint once more at swimming blood cells, or test a urine for sugar. There were no sophisticated dipsticks then: the tests were all done with primary cooking over a smelly bunsen burner.

Phone calls would come up from the Casualty Department. Were they really for us, or one of the specialist wards? Beds were always short and there would be intertelephoning to see where there was a space. By the time our beds-in-the-middle were filled, our hands were tied. When the patients came up there would be bustle. All the hospital trolleys had their individual groan or limp, and the powers-that-be calculated that they were always a few inches wider than a half-swing door so two people were necessary to manoeuvre them in and behind the screens. Then a history had to be taken – from the patient, if conscious, from an accompanying relation or often an accompanying policeman. Occasionally the constable would sit there, as a sort of tether, a boring job if ever there was one, usually a kind man, but often not very good in the presence of blood. If his charge was much battered, and actual physical restraint were not necessary, he would slump to the floor in a swoon, and we would have to step over his long blue legs until someone strong came along to heave him to safety and revive him with tea.

Patients not unconscious, roaring drunk or deranged were often desperately apprehensive. There was a lot more to do than just examine their condition, and this was when we learned most. Possibly they were reassured by finding 'ordinary people' as well as nurses there to talk to, or to rant at: we were certainly sustained by them. If all was quiet and in order, the medicals would all retire to the duty room and play Monopoly with restrained frenzy. Then, just when you had acquired that Mayfair hotel and two houses on the Angel, the phone would ring again.

About three o'clock in the morning, when night pressures really seemed to ease, we would stagger out into the sleeping winter town, dead black and empty, with little pools of light, frequently blowing hard or sleeting, sometimes squeaking underfoot with new snow. In summer, there would be that feeling of caught breath, as early morning slowly penetrated the city with a translucence behind the columns on Calton Hill. A passing car would seem like a juggernaut, so empty were the streets. The long trail home on foot, fortunately downhill, after a hectic night would be broken by a hot pie and a mug of tea at an all-night food stall at the bottom of the Mound. There we might find a very different set of clients, who were unaware of time or place, or young revellers homing from a dance, to whom we felt infinitely superior. Those were secret nights, thinking back, some of the most worthwhile ever spent. You could walk all over the town in the night then, and never look over your shoulder, watching the dawn slowly silvering the waters of the Forth, and the hills of Fife beginning to swim blue against the northern sky.

XI   LIGHT AT THE END

The next stage was to see how people lived outside the hospital
walls. We learned treatment in the community by dispensary
practice. The dispensaries themselves were established in a more
spacious age, on charitable foundations, distributed through the
town in places that had once been strategic. With central housing
being forced out in favour of commerce, they were now often
distant from those they served. Aesthetically they were a glimpse
of a previous leisured century. Polished shelves surmounted by
beautiful glass jars with gilded tops and gold leaf labels, detailing
MIST IPECAC CO and MIST PERTUSSIS in fine Roman capitals.
Underneath were rows of little drawers holding instruments and
pills. Occasionally we would be requested to make up our own
pills of varying mixtures, grinding the powders in a mortar and
then rolling them on a circular lipped board. It was an art to get
the right consistency that would stick together and contain the
right dosage. Sometimes they looked like miniature marbles, the
kind small boys flicked among the cobblestones.

   The dispensary was presided over by a general practitioner who
would attend at certain times, and we were called out by message,
often brought by a little shivering girl, or an ill-written smudge on
a torn piece of paper with a very doubtful address was thrust
through the letter slit. We then set out to look for the source of
the call.

   It is difficult to reconstitute these houses. Some were relics of the splendours of the original New Town, in the upper reaches of Leith Walk and old St James's Square. Penetrating a stinking common stair and a long unlit passage, you eventually might find the right door, unlabelled. We were armed with a tiny torch for peering down throats, and its wavering light barely reached the high ceiling, but would just show a civic plaque over the door, announcing the number of persons supposed to be living there.

On entry, it was often icy and usually overpopulated, smelling of old clothes, illness, chill, desperation, punctuated by coughs or infant wails. Older children were often pathetically silent. Illness brought out the supportive crowd. Under dark and chill conditions we made our examination and considered diagnosis. If apparently straightforward, we asked someone reliable in the house to come back with us for medicine. If we were in doubt, we said we would get a 'specialist' to attend, the general practitioner on call.

At that time, fevers were rampant, and many of these cases were young children. Scarlatina, measles, whooping cough, the dreaded diphtheria, bronchitis and pneumonia; tuberculosis and rheumatic fever and violent diarrhoea were also recurrent horrors. Under such conditions of infection, the only answer was to send them to Fever Hospital to protect the remaining swarm of family, and the waifs would be swathed in a blanket and taken off there, rarely seeing their mother again until certified free, but woefully wan. Survival of the fittest indeed: few would be considered fit in the light of the present day. We brought home large and voracious fleas, and dreaded catching scabies or collecting bed bugs.

A ghastly slum survived intact into the Fifties. Crammed together in the lee of Calton Hill, where the sun rarely reached and the rain ran down the hill and flooded the cobbles, lay Greenside. The green was weed-green, slime-green, fungus-green, damp-wall-green. Tenements there shared one lavatory for eight dwellings. One house I entered contained only a shiny wireless set and a bare bed on whose bare mattress lay a naked woman, far gone with pneumonia, covered only by a soldier's overcoat. When I lifted it, bugs scuttled and fleas jumped. Rent men called on this paradise weekly, and those who did not pay were evicted, their homes usually reoccupied by nightfall. There were many slums like this then, known apparently only to the Poor Law medical services, the rent man, and the inhabitants.

Some years later a maniac drowned two little children in one of the lavatories, which had better be left undescribed. This agitated the authorities sufficiently to condemn the whole place, and pull down their civic shame.

Lectures started in the mornings again, some memorable, most not. We learned from the personalities of the lecturers, sometimes repeaters of rote, sometimes true eccentrics. One produced superb, finished verbal essays on the medical condition of obliging patients whom he miraculously put at ease on a dusty platform in a chalky lecture theatre. Another got into trouble, as he kept describing tumours resembling 'large tennis balls' or 'small golf balls'. Eventually he received a terse note from the Athletic Association saying that his similes were unacceptable, so he switched to likening them to fruit, which possessed variables. But none of us forgot his statement: "She was not a woman with a tumour, but a tumour with a woman! " He told us of 'a witch' in his youth who lived in a wood, and they used to hear her howling. Later it was discovered that she suffered from a urethral caruncle, an inflamed and sensitive knob. The howls were of pure pain, when she left her hut to urinate in the bushes.

The practical work for this professor was midwifery. He was a splendid figure with a gently curving frontal elevation and horn-rimmed pince-nez which hung on a wide ribbon. These were adjusted to look at you, should you ask a question. His phraseology was precise, and his lectures always memorable.

We had to live in a hostel for a period. Night and day a bell would ring, and we would all have to dress and belt up a hill to the maternity hospital, where we were summoned to an 'abnormal' case. In the intervals we would go in and be initiated in the management of normal cases, and, with luck, do the delivery itself. We were taught to wait — 'masterly inactivity' was the term used. The mother took her own time and it was not the rule to help by inductions or episiotomy until real need arose. It is amazing how well nature collaborated.

Birth forceps are built with two separate interlocking blades: they are thus easy to sterilise, but as difficult for a novice to assemble as the first unfolding of a deck-chair. We practised with these in the cold, on a dummy woman with a tightly fitting dummy baby, but the textures of both felt terribly wrong, and were not reassuring. If we were first in the rush to abnormal cases, we might be lucky enough to deal with them in vivo. The women concerned, I must add, were all well anaesthetised at times like this, and experts stood firmly at our elbow, so rescue was always at hand, and the patient was unaware of the novice.

Antenatal clinics were elementary then, and thus we had far more 'abnormal' cases to deal with. The mother with childhood rickets might show a deformed pelvis, and this provoked horrifying difficulties in delivery.

My brother-in-law, who had grown up in France, took his maternity training there and evidently antenatal examination was a regular thing in Paris in the early Twenties. He gave us a graphic description of a roomful of parous ladies at different stages sitting round the wall, naked except for pink corsets but retaining their hats — a Toulouse-Lautrec vision.

The maternity wards in 1936/37 were hardly models of comfort, and in moral Edinburgh distinctions were then made. Mothers blessed with a wedding ring received their surnames. Those without were called by Christian names only. Thus was official virtue preserved, but the treatment itself was identical.

When we were working in the Labour Ward, Europe was agog waiting for the birth of an heir to the Dutch throne. Souvenir potters everywhere had issued commemorative plates with the expected month and year, and the month was rapidly running out. Every labouring lady was bidden to push and 'beat Queen Juliana', who fortunately gave birth to the then Princess Beatrix with minutes to spare before the end of the month. Perhaps a deputation of the potters had been waiting in desperation in the hall of the palace.

After dealing with ten normal hospital cases, and having peered behind many backs at 'abnormals', we were each released with a midwife into the town. We lived two at a time in special lodgings, and I used to rush to the phone trying to beat an Arab medical youth wearing a nocturnal hairnet. Hospital deliveries were not de rigueur then, and antenatal examination not a regular commitment. Besides, there were many girls 'surprised' by impending birth pangs. A taxi was provided and we went off into the night to an unknown address on the receipt of a doubtful message to meet the midwife, occasionally to be confronted by a situation of horror. One could then only call for an ambulance, rushing round the streets to find a telephone box, and wait, praying, and attempting an authoritative calm with knocking knees. Usually Granny was there, a sheet anchor. Husbands seemed to need more treatment than wives.

Some of these memories are gilded. A girl in a box bed, a fire in the grate winking over polished brass, an eternally singing kettle ready with hot water, a padded clothes basket awaiting its occupant. Nothing can improve on the feeling of communion on these occasions when natural processes proceed naturally. The labouring woman, the calm and caring midwife, the 'doctor' in the shape of a student attempting to staunch her own state of petrifaction, and a granny who has seen it all before. When all was over, the little red squaller cleared of mucus, the cord cut, the child wiped and secure in its basket, the third stage with the after-birth safely delivered, peace descended like a benison. Granny produced a pot of thick black tea, and biscuits, and the four of us — a new mother and three rude mechanicals — felt as if we had climbed Everest and come down again. One single-end in Leith gave me a precious present: their sole decoration, a collage of a thistle made from shiny chocolate wrappers.

The statistician today would consider these methods ripe for disaster. I can remember two difficult situations. One was an abnormally slow labour, and I said that I should like to call out the tutor. On hearing his name, a man she had been roughly examined by in hospital, the patient let out a shriek, started pushing hard and ripped herself, rather than have him back. Fortunately the stitches I put in held, and subsequent visits revealed a comfortable and contented mum with a robust boy. She was especially overjoyed as she had previously lost one ovary through surgery, and had three daughters already. She had been in despair over this pregnancy: her man had said he only wanted a laddie, and she thought that her remaining ovary produced girls only. She had a real bonus.

We were supposed to return to hospital with the afterbirth

swathed in newspapers, to be sure it was complete. In another ill-equipped home, I put it in its wrappings under the bed, as we had to resuscitate the baby. In the interval the husband came in with his huge Alsatian dog, which immediately made for such a prize and fled with it through the door. The front door was open, and for about ten minutes I rushed about in a wet dawn in a depressing housing scheme trying to catch a playful dog and its bundle. Finally he disappeared, gulping. A disastrous night's work, but the baby survived. It did not seem a very happy family, but there were not many about in that quarter of the town.

Visiting afterwards, we got close to these women, and heard some sensational goings on in the realms of matrimony, which we had been brought up to believe was a safe haven. They longed to talk to someone, and that was a valuable piece of training for us. Our respect for our patients grew further.

Many of our contemporaries went for their practical work to Dublin, and brought even more hair-raising tales of the less inhibited Irish mothers. They learned as a matter of course to secrete cottonwool blobs soaked with ether on their persons against generalised flea attacks, and talked of the difficulties of lighting in homes where there wasn't any. Frequently the only illumination was a tiny lamp burning in from of the Blessed Virgin, which they had to use despite frantic protests from patients fearing divine thunderbolts.

In psychiatry the infinite fascinations of the human mind revealed themselves: such normal *people,* suddenly flying into a fantasy of dream, of paranoia, of total delusion. We felt as if we were chasing ghosts. The clinics, therefore, were especially enthralling, and humiliated us by our impotence in investigating man's mind. Visiting the hospital, we were often greeted by a tall kilted figure playing the bagpipes by the gate, a gallant officer who had developed delusions, but there was nothing deluded about his welcome. The sharpsighted though would perceive that, instead of the skean dhu pushed in his stocking, there was a pencil.

One memorable and intelligent lady told us an academic story. She had been involved in writing a doctoral thesis on an obscure German poet. This had been passed by her professor. In the last stages she discussed it with him, and he had condemned the whole enterprise outright, without appeal. In a state of dire persecution, she had appealed to the Vice-Chancellor, her M.P., the Queen, passers-by, and anyone who looked helpful in the Midlands where she had studied, and was ultimately sent for residential mental treatment in the north, her home base. She proved extremely useful to our psychiatry professor, living quietly and translating European papers into English for him. If she were not reminded of her primary interests, all was well. I can still visualise her grey hair, her keen glasses, her extremely lucid exposition until her voice rose in execration of her detested detractor. He was the psychiatric case, she insisted. Was she right?

In later years, I served on a University Committee where the question of overseeing of theses came up, and we were able, with some persuasion backed by other academics who had come across the same obstructionism, to ensure that an additional umpire was necessary in judging a Ph.D. thesis. Too often the academic mind runs into objections of its own devising, and can cancel out a budding line of new thought. One of our daughters, at her university, was later told by a well-known academic, "It is facts we want; this is not the place for ideas." This remark was made by a psychologist . . . . .

Our final training year was spent under the gathering shadow following Munich. No one could really believe in Chamberlain's little bit of paper, yet we clung to it to avoid taking in the horror that could not be borne. It made us work a lot harder, as we had the certainty of knowing that we would be needed.

There was less and less time for beer and skittles. The first years had produced dances, ward parties, celebrations for the win of a fellow undergraduate's greyhound − alas it had to be sold to pay his racing debts − and various cultural side issues. A small group of us used solemnly to write poetry or essays on chosen subjects and discuss them together. On Thursdays the Reid Orchestra used to rehearse in the mornings in the Usher Hall for the evening concerts under Sir Donald Tovey, and we often sneaked into the back and listened ecstatically, sometimes with a score from the library. A special delight was when the Busch brothers came, Wilhelm and Adolf. Having expressed their disgust with the growing National

Socialist policies in Berlin, where I used to listen to them in the Conservatorium in 1932, they had moved to Switzerland. There were also weekly choir practices.

My father was having recurrent depressive attacks, and my mother developed glaucoma and shingles simultaneously, so between classes I had to dash home to administer eye drops and dry dressings. It seemed at the time that sitting exams was quite out of the question, but youth is infinitely elastic and sleep isn't a problem. Fate was kind: we sweated through our last hurdles, including crash courses of 'specials'. Eyes, Ears, Nose and Throat, further psychiatry, veneral diseases and fevers, and, at last, in the best days of summer, we scribbled through a week and a half of Finals, followed by vivas. These were nerve-wracking. The best advice I had was to think what the examiner would look like as a patient himself, or in his bath. This produced enough inner levity to lighten natural despair. Besides, we felt, it is 1939 and war is coming. They will need us.

Once the Finals list was up, there was a day of total euphoria — then the next step immediately raised its head. War was imminent, and we had to start really learning our trade. We made a list of the chiefs we had worked for, and bombarded them for testimonials. They responded with great generosity, considering how little they can have known us; only years later do you realise what value to put on these pieces of paper, but to the recipient they seem rose-coloured. Our beloved surgical chief was sick unto death, and his second-in-command was already drafted into the Army so we could importune neither of them. I had spent a lot of time working on a project for an Orthopaedics prize, for which there can have been little competition. Apart from some cash, the cachet was a residency in the equivalent hospital. When I approached this chief to claim it, having done a lot of work with him as a student, he said with a shake of the head that alas it was impossible to implement. Ladies were not considered strong enough. He knew that I had heaved heavies in plaster beds and on metal frames in a former occupation, but this was not convincing. Besides, that residency only contained lavatory accommodation for gentlemen, which ruled it out conclusively. Such were the reasons of the time.

A PICTURE OF HEALTH

A first job had to be arranged smartly, or they would all be taken up. Fate was kind again. An experienced Dutch graduate who had been taken on as surgical houseman in the Sick Children's Hospital, was called back to his own country's defence in due course. I went to see the Chief, Gertrude Herzfeld, an eminent woman who worked with brilliance and compassion. Having fought her way up through the male hierarchy, she knew the difficulties, and had been the first woman to take her seat in the Royal College of Surgeons of Edinburgh. With a German name, work in the First World War had not been easy, and she had matured through sheer grit and experience. She regarded my nursing experience with children as a bonus and opened the door to a job usually given to someone more senior.

With the guarantee of employment, Jim and I reapproached my father. His head was still full of old enmities and what the world had lost, so it was not easy for him, in a state of deep depression, to accept our belief in each other. He had financed me for five highly expensive years, on a small pension. But we were both qualified, theoretically able to earn in a professional job, and he allowed us to announce our engagement after five years of waiting, which we celebrated on our graduation day. Having disapproved of those loved by his daughters, fortunately he lived to bless both sons-in-law.

We had an emotional farewell with the janitor of the Medical Quad, Mr Forge, who had been infinitely accommodating. For lectures we had had to give in name cards; by these means the authorities checked whether you had been present. It was a ridiculous system, merely protecting bad lecturers, as good ones filled their theatres without trouble, so many of us had a little modest fun. Among our number was an older, kind and delightful earl with a double title. He wrote B and S to stand for his earldoms, so there were comics who wrote C and A, X and Y, and other witticisms. Mr Forge would give us a look and check us as identified and then we might slink off. He was one of a group of splendid ex-military gents, well-used to idiot rookies, and they treated us with benevolence. A greeting from their top-hatted, silver-buttoned figures made our day. In this state of dottiness, we reeled out into the real world, a very different place.

Graduation day is a deeply moving occasion. The Hippocratic Oath is such a binding expression of integrity it cannot be otherwise, and, standing among over a hundred of your fellows each with hand upraised, swearing to honour it, you share its communal Credo with reverence. Afterwards, we drove round the town in an open horse-drawn cab, wearing our gowns and hoods, circling twice round the policeman then directing traffic at the bottom of the Mound, a delightful avuncular figure called Bernard, whom we had got to know well throughout the years. He stopped his traffic and embraced us both.

SICK CHILDREN

XII   LOOKING IN: ANOTHER WAR

To begin with, we revelled in reaction. Life became a total blank,
sleeping and sleeping, walking, swimming, reading every irrelevant
work available, and getting away from town.

We both drove down to London in August to attend our clinical
tutor's wedding at the Savoy Chapel, and then went to *Goodbye,
Mr Chips,* a real nostalgic weepie. The weather was brilliant, the
sky already filled with glittering barrage balloons, a protection
against the expected rogue aircraft. All the traffic lights were
reduced to slits, and we shot through quite a few with inaccuracy
until we recognised this. As can be deduced, traffic was thinner
then.

I came back to Edinburgh to an empty house and, on Sunday
3rd September, when the family were still away, by chance I
turned on the radio to hear the uncanny voice of Neville Chamberlain announcing that Germany had invaded Poland and that we
were at war. Almost at once the siren began to wail, implying, as
we had been told, air attack. I rushed down to the basement
kitchen, filled the stone sink to put out any hypothetical fire,
and sat with my back against a good solid stone wall until the
steady note of the All Clear sounded. It was the first cry of Wolf,
but, barring childbirth, the loneliest moment in my life.

We were instructed about blackout, so I heaved myself through
a tiny transom in a lofty bathroom roof with a can of
black paint to obscure the skylights, and then made black curtains

for the whole house. These had to have poppers on so they did not gape. All the shops were running out of the right material, and it was quite a scramble.

Eventually some of the family came home, so at least there was company. At nights the streets were entirely black; the cars crawled on tiny cracks of headlamp, and the pedestrians had down-held torches, with their bulbs swathed in red paper. Later you learned a sort of sonar, avoiding figures and lamp-posts. It was a mystical world, peopled with ghosts who passed you like a breath.

Thanking Fate for a job to go and *do* something, I moved needs and books up to the Sick Children's Hospital.

The plunge took my breath away. A long ward full of cots with an external balcony held patients from newly born up to eleven years old. On the balcony, swathed in jackets, blankets, woolly gloves and hats, lay the 'chesty' patients, blue, bronchial or newly diagnosed tuberculous. Oxygen tents were not in use then. We held a glass funnel attached to a heavy cylinder over the patient's nose and mouth if such emergency was needed, but the enforced oxygenation of Edinburgh's winter climated contributed its part. The children hardly needed to exert their breathing muscles — the brisk air did it for them

The surgical range was huge. The tiniest babies were there with congenital deformities, from hare lips to missing parts. Gertrude Herzfeld, the Chief, a large woman with hands to match and a steady all-absorbing eye of immense kindness, dealt with an infant of a few days with a non-functioning cystic duct, a tube normally barely perceptible and half a centimetre long. By microscopic manoeuvring and without today's visual aids, she constructed a new one which worked. Babies with persistent projectile vomiting due to duodenal stricture were gently tied to a board with outstretched arms, and very lightly sedated. The ward sister sat beside this tiny crucifixion, her pinkie in a fingerstall dipped in honey, which the baby sucked. Local anaesthetic was elegantly injected over the little hard lump showing the duodenal contracture, the skin opened and the muscle exposed. Three small nicks in it eased the tension, and the skin was closed. Within a few minutes the sleeping babe, contented and still smelling of honey,

103

was returned to its cot, and later that evening had its first total meal. It was an oft-repeated miracle.

Plastic surgery was also constant. Facial deformity was self-explanatory, actual malformation such as hare lip and cleft palate which could extend into the nose, or the hideous stains of 'port wine' type, eventually needing skin grafts. Sexual malformation was a surprise. Children of indefinite sex anatomically often came from afar, some having been firmly labelled at birth by the midwife and reared as such even when they patently differed. Medicine had not heard of chromosomes then; what to do when Jessie aged 8 came down from the Highlands with her parents, and was indubitably Jamie, misshapen? Habit, repute, locality, attitudes, all came into consideration before remodelling, and the association of the child with its siblings, its former life, and what it would return to. In some cases emigration post-operatively helped the situation, rather than returning to a small village and its finger-pointing gossips. Sex was not a subject for discussion then, outside the consulting-room. Refugees from the wrong gender were not infrequent, and few gave them any help, surely one of the loneliest positions conceivable. Until Jan Morris took up the challenge and wrote *Conundrum* in the Seventies, few persons believed in it. It must be remembered that hospitals collected these cases; they were scattered sparingly in the community.

What would Solomon do in this field?

I remembered a girl who had come into the gynaecological ward, a handsome twenty-year-old. She reported that her periods had stopped, her breasts were shrinking, she was getting hairier. Emotionally, she had lost affection for her sailor fiancé. When checking her blood pressure, I saw it suddenly leap as she was gazing at a plump and seductive young nurse. Her sexual urges were changing course. The surgeons had made a diagnosis of tumour of the adrenal, the gland having hormonal influence. Both glands were unavailaingly examined and no other cause could be found. She had to be discharged, unhelped, to what I imagine would be eventual suicide. We recognised no way past the two sex barriers at that time. We know a little more nowadays but are still slow at recognising the great personal isolation in these conditions.

Children, ill, can terrify. In less than hours a robust and beefy infant can become a tiny, shrunken, whimpering bundle. This may primarily be due to loss of fluid, but the cause must be found with immediacy, and babies cannot give you information as to site. Telescoping bowels, obstructions, infected ears, medical causes, infections, have to be sorted out, and to the houseman blearily woken in the night after twenty-four hours of continuous activity, it is a major crisis. There is a waiting surgeon to be rung up, and symptoms to be clearly described before directions are given − either careful watching, passive treatment, masterly inactivity under constant observation, or instant preparation of the theatre, while guarding the patient from further shock. With a child deteriorating before your eyes, there is no emergency to match it.

The other horrifiers were burns, scalds, and osteomyelitis, where infection settles in a bone, producing intense local pain, fever and toxaemia. In my first fortnight on the ward, three little boys came in with fulminating osteomyelitis, and they all died in a few days. Antibiotics were not known then, to cope. The sobbing mother of one had just lost her husband in the Ark Royal, an early naval casualty in the Orkneys, and she was now losing their only child. I sobbed beside her, there was no way of avoiding it, and afterwards she actually said that it had helped − a shared release, I suppose. I know that after this triad of tragedy I went down to Jim and cried and cried − I didn't know how to go back to hospital, which appeared to give us no help to give to others. Once grief is freed, strength comes creeping in again in a rewarding tide, and experience begins to back it.

Burns and scalds were horrific, the pain and shock unnerving. They were so often avoidable, resulting from thoughtless parents rather than careless children: the child that had sat in a frying-pan newly set on the floor, the child whose father had dipped its feet in boiling water to warm them, so that the skin pulled off like socks, the child with the unmistakable signature of a hot poker on its leg. We had to cut off sticking clothes and dead skin, paint them with gentian violet against infection, and silver nitrate to protect the bared flesh from the air, and they were then nursed naked under a cone of electric lights to keep their temperature steady. Skin took months to grow, despite grafting, and always seemed too tight for a growing child. Periods in hospital could be endless, or were often repeated.

An Italian boy came in with a sore on his chin which he had scratched. This had become infected, and his whole face swelled into a scabrous melon. We could only watch, helpless, the infection spreading until toxaemia stilled his brain. His death was followed by an invasion of shrieking relatives into the ward, terrifying all the other little inmates and asserting that if only he had been sent to the Royal Infirmary, he would now be home and cured. For a houseman who had sat up most of the night with him after a long day, this was training in psychology at a very fundamental level.

The boy had been so ill on entry that we had been unable to identify the infective organism, and I was detailed to get a specimen of heart blood when he was in the mortuary. This was an appalling commission, but oddly brought its own healing. Dead children lay tenderly in their white shrouds, their hands clasped round a flower that kept its life in their cold grasp, peace on their faces. A kind and thoughtful hand had covered the wall and ceiling with frescoes of children and flowers in an eternal meadow. You realised that the heaviest strain had been taken by the nurses aged eighteen or so, who had made their charges fit and ready for their eternal peace. Even poor Giulio's face seemed to have subsided, and be sleeping. The pictures on the walls are now covered with curtains 'in case they upset the parents', so I have been told.

Parents were allowed into the wards only twice a week in those days, so our free time was spent with the children in as far as we were able. Otherwise they would have felt quite deserted.

'Keep a stiff upper lip,' we were told by the outsiders. One's upper lip is rarely a problem; it is the lower one has to bite. This muscular inaccuracy was perpetuated last century by a Miss Phoebe Cary, and has entered mythology.

> "And though hard be the task,
> Keep a stiff upper lip,"

she wrote. Can her brother have been advertising his new moustache?

LOOKING IN: ANOTHER WAR

Outside was the 'Cold War'. Cold was a doubly operative word as one of the chilliest of winters set in. The continent of Europe was darkening in every news bulletin, and we sat waiting, wondering what would hit us. We weren't very well informed on emergency: when a lone German plane appeared trying to bomb the Forth Bridge, we all sat beside the huge north window of the operating theatre, watching the bursts in the sky, and celebrating its departure in cold tea. Food was rationed out. At Monday breakfast, we each had our labelled dish of two ounces of butter for the week. One robust resident, used to having such a ration on one slice of toast, peered round his *Times* every morning bugeyed at each plate, wondering if there was an extra scrape.

After an operating day starting at 8.30, dragging ourselves into the dining-room at 4 p.m., we would find a small slice of soggy bread and cold baked beans. We were on duty forty-eight hours at a stretch. When we did escape in an evening, fixing with another houseman to double up, we had a freezing black walk across the large open space of the Meadows, clutching a newly-issued gas mask, before reaching the comparative security of a tram. The city was full of men who had taken the King's Shilling and were waiting for call-up. The intervening time was used for their refreshment, which often went too far. To avoid embroilment, flat rather than fleet of foot, dodging the drunks was often a tricky process, but they were not at their quickest either. It was a freezing winter, and snow lay long, shedding a little light of its own when the stars shone through, so at least one could tell direction in the all-pervading black. On the return journey, the only figures about were the Air Raid Wardens looking for tell-tale cracks of light as people went to their beds. The night seemed so short it had hardly started before we were in the theatre again.

We worked for board and bed, no pay cheques. By searching case notes, we could find early incidence of T.B. in some of our patients, which statisticians wanted. For this information they paid one shilling per head. During my six months on duty I dug up thirty of these, and received my thirty pieces of silver, enough to cover the tram fares — the first earned medical money.

'Treats' were to have a home to take refuge in for an hour or two once or twice a week, and a chocolate bar from her rations from the mother of a child for whom a series of splints were made. Such is the importance of tiny memories in a dark, bewildering and exhausting period.

THE LAND MINE

XIII   VILLAGE AT BAY

March 1940 came, still apparently a long hard winter, and an SOS
from my sister in Suffolk. Her husband, the local doctor, had been
called up, thanks to his juvenile services as a sixteen-year-old in
World War I, and an aged retired gentleman had moved in as a
substitute who was now gravely ill. Was I conceivably free? The
practice was still clotted with mortgage, and no one was available
to take on a rustic area at no notice. A friend qualifying in surgery
took on the last month of my hospital residency, and I sped south,
raw as beef but rich in enthusiasm. There was even money to be
earned. Locums at that time were classified as worth £1 a day and
their keep, but owing to practice difficulties and my inexperience,
we agreed on half this figure. The patients weren't consulted.

   East Anglia then was almost an island. There was little general
transport, and the roads wound round and round and round,
eventually leading you near to where you first started. In normal
times it was common to see signposts directing you to the same
village in opposite directions, but by now they had begun to be
removed to puzzle an invading enemy, and this did not help
geography. The countryside was largely given over to the part-
ridge-shooting gentry for a few weeks of the year and lay fallow
the rest of the time, with straggling hedges and choked ditches.
The farmers were usually impoverished tenants, surviving with
little capital to improve their land, the beautiful old farmhouses
damp and decrepit.

A PICTURE OF HEALTH

Villages and hamlets were contained, intermarried and related, but our village was long and straggling. One end was Church, and this edifice stood squarely behind the house; the other was Chapel. In the middle of the village street was a tiny room devoted to the Plymouth Brethren, of whom there were a handful. They seemed almost to belong to the founding fathers and dressed like the Mennonites. My relatives had to drive eight miles for their Roman Catholic rites.

Our home was historically interesting, in that a Chapel blacksmith had once lived in it who had murdered his inamorata in the kitchen by setting fire to her with a lamp. We did in fact have a blacksmith at that time who looked capable of following the same example, and had a Reputation. "His loins do burn," my brother-in-law used to say, in Suffolk tongue.

The surgery opened off the sitting-room and had a tiny porch with a bench on which visiting patients perched. Behind it was an icy room with slate shelves and a bucket − the dispensary. There was an oil lamp to work with, and a can of hot water was carried in from the kitchen stove, which at that time was a sturdy 'Florence' composed of three tin cylinders with lights at the bottom, running on paraffin. The nearest chemist was five miles away, and our country radius covering patients reached as far, and further, so one had to be prepared.

My dear sister was always a brave woman, and she had explained to patients that 'the doctor's sister-in-law was a doctor too.' In an inter-related community this was accepted with bovine calm.

My first patient was a roadman, rarely an articulate profession. He merely dropped his trousers, turned his back, and revealed a group of piles like a bunch of grapes. I learned that this was a fairly frequent cause for visitations. Indoor water was unknown in most dwellings, a water closet as unattainable as the Ritz. You walked through the mud of the garden path to the Shed. In winter, this was icy and black, in summer humming with blue-bottles. Neither eventuality could be greeted with the joy 'The Specialist' wrote about so feelingly, with the view through his half-open door to distract him. It was something to be avoided until dire need and pressure precipitated the painful condition

110

presented. You couldn't call it a 'convenience'.

Old Mr Burgess, in his seventies, had been bedbound for some years, his wife, in her eighties, climbing the ladder-like stair to his room on her swollen ankles several times a day. My brother-in-law knew him well. With disapproval of his ignorance of 'Woman's Lot', I examined the old gentleman thoroughly, read what notes there were, and could find no sign or reason for prolonged rest at the expense of his wife. We had a cheerful conversation, and I persuaded him of the joys of spring outside, and all he could watch from his cottage door. We even got him dressed, and down his ladder, and I went off feeling a pioneer for easier living all round. The day after he was still downstairs, so I did not go back for a fortnight, but the next visit revealed him back in his ill-smelling bed, and his wife sucking her tea by the fire. She said he wasn't so well, and it was easier if he stayed in his bed. Feeling affronted at such disregard of well-meaning action, I stumped up his stair and asked him what he meant by it.

"Well you see, Lidy-doctor," (the village's usual form of address) "I always do feel bad for some weeks after me bowels move," he replied. Apparently this event occurred once a fortnight and bedrest was necessary in preparation for, and convalescence from it. My predecessor knew this: I didn't. It taught me not to try to interfere with old customs that worked, or long-established marriages.

Most of our patients were deeply rural: farm workers; the village shopkeepers; the men from the local spade and shovel works; the vicar and his family, a genial soul on first name terms with most of the neighbourhood, who had a daughter married to a tenant farmer; the miller and his handsome sons, usually dusted with meal from the windmill up the hill; the squire and his vigorous old mother who had never had her authority questioned (she gave me a china chamber pot to help with First Aid in case of invasion). Some landed gentry who tended to use the doctor as a facility rather than an essential need became very attached. One aged eighty-three flailed about with a tough walking-stick and told me how at the age of thirteen she had been warned that she wouldn't live very long, as the wall of her heart was too thin. It was wearing well and beat like a gong, but she still produced it as a symptom, over hoarded China tea and cucumber sandwiches. She had quarrelled with the other doctors who had made so bold as to doubt her word.

The squire still exercised his village prerogatives, and we had some disagreement. He demanded that all able-bodied men left in the village joined his Local Defence Volunteers (Churchill had just adjured us all to fight on the beaches). I tried unavailingly to nobble some as stretcher-bearers and First Aid personnel for the inhabitants when the invasion came, which we were informed was a possibility. East Anglia bulged out into the North Sea in a tempting fashion, offering a flat coast to the enemy map-readers, by then in growing possession of the Netherlands.

During the day the Battle of Britain roared overhead, tiny silver savaging dots in the sky, attacking the stravaiging German bombers. We heard unpleasant rumours of children being struck by descending metal bits in playgrounds, and the local baker's van was peppered by a hedge-hopper. We saw the bullet holes to prove it. We kept being told that the enemy's eyes and ears were everywhere, so that official news was scarce. The local paper told us guardedly to watch for potato blight (one wondered if this was spread in the night by the marauders), or gave us a dramatic account of the village maidens' weddings. "The bride wore saxe blue with lemon yellow accessories and red roses." White was expensive on clothes coupons, and not always deserved.

Midwifery cases punctuated the usual routine. A man would arrive in the night on a bicycle from some cottage across the fields. His wife had rarely informed doctor or midwife of her expectation, and sometimes was apparently unaware herself. He would just say she was took bad. One either had to follow him back, or load his bike into the car and follow his directions on dipped headlights, which was not easy as bicycles go where cars cannot. At the final decanting, a veiled torch was not always sufficient to show up the cow-pats, unless it was raining.

Indoors, the woman either lay in the Room, or you climbed a ladder to a chilly attic, the ties supporting the eaves so low that you sometimes had to crawl underneath. Bringing hot water up was quite a feat, and you had to manoeuvre a bag as well: trustfully you relied on the man, the gran, or the midwife if she had also managed to find her way after being telephoned for from our surgery. Country phones were non-existent. In England, the midwife usually preceded the doctor, who often left her to it. In the north, we had been trained to turn up promptly, for which I was deeply grateful.

The woman accepted her labour, the first or the fifth, as a totally normal process, rather differently from the town ladies we had previously met, with their sophisticated demands for chloroform. It was infinitely isolated, in the middle of inaccessible countryside. If anything had gone wrong, if hospitalisation had been required, this was thirty miles away. Trust in the Lord and his remarkable handiwork kept us going, and we went. Only when it was all over and you realised how near crisis you had been did deflation set in, but the Granny's tea brewed from the water from the green pond outside the door did its magic best, and no stronger spirits could have been more satisfying.

The night after one particularly racking episode, just as sleep had come, the phone went and the Squire's familiar bark came down it. Would I come at once? His maid, Emmie, had frightful stomach ache. She said she had been eating gooseberries, but he was convinced it was an appendix and was very worried. His Squiress and their children had been evacuated and he was living uneasily in a large and chilly house. Emmie was the standby.

When I arrived, the Squire in his dressing-gown was restoring himself with a glass of something strong and showed me up. We were greeted by a volley of shrill barking and a vibrating squall. The Squiress's Pekinese dog was on guard by Emmie's bed, while on it lay the surfeit of gooseberries, a well-formed newborn male, proving positive life. Emmie had to lean out and calm the dog and hand him to the Squire before I could approach. He was then sent post-haste for the midwife who had no transport at that time, while I set to.

Between us all we achieved some order, the infant Samuel being the easiest to deal with. I asked Emmie for his origins. To the end she averred immaculate conception; only after long thought she admitted she had met a man once at a village dance, and talked to him at the door. She was quite unmoved, and quite prepared to cook the Squire's breakfast in the morning. I pondered blackmailing some of my stretcher-bearers back from him, but thought better of it.

The Local Defence Volunteers were a stoic bunch. No weapons were available at those early days, and they paraded with wickedly sharpened broomsticks. They were accustomed to using hayforks, so these were held out at the ready. Britain was short of metal, and we were all asked to give what we could find, so gardens lost their railings, and rubbish-dumps their old bedsprings and saucepans. A cartoon in *Punch* showed an aeroplane flying with a frying-pan shaped hole in it, to show that one of us had been selfish. Later Mussolini, in the same state of mind, asked the Italian wives for their wedding rings, and got them. We stuck at saucepans, I am glad to say.

Collections of scrap metal were assembled in piles across certain roads, in order to prevent the enemy invading the flat fields of Anglia, until they were claimed, supposedly to build new aircraft with. These piles were manned by the Volunteers in shifts, with their broomsticks. As the Duke of Wellington remarked of his troops, "I don't know what effect these men will have upon the enemy, but, by God, they terrify me."

Driving along a flat road running over a flat moor, I was denied progress by a pile of junk and this defence force. A small piece of typescript had been issued by the local military authority, in purple carbon, saying, "This is Dr H. Please let him filter through this barrier." There was some head-scratching over this, but regardless of gender, they shifted two iron bedheads and a field gate and waved me on. The first radar discs had been put up in our vicinity, but we had been told they harboured 'death rays', and you held your breath as you went past with averted eyes. The ostrich is a cleverer bird than we think. Later in the year petrol became very scarce and I developed calves of iron on an old pushbike. A handsome neighbouring doctor developed a seat of iron on a horse, and he just rode round obstructions on the roadway with a wave of the hand. Presumably an invading tank might have been similarly inspired. Britain had been surrounding her coastline with great concrete dragons' teeth, and the flat beaches were spiked against air landings. We felt safer, as if we had put up wire against the neighbour's children's footballs.

VILLAGE AT BAY

After the débacle of Dunkirk rumours grew thick and fast, and pressure on preserving children increased. America's generous heart leapt into action. We read a notice that readers of the *Boston Transcript* were preparing to receive our children into care until safety was re-established. My sister's son was then eleven and her daughter nine. The latter, with her sharp Catholic's eye, had noticed two nuns in the town where she was at school sitting with their knees crossed, a posture unknown to the Religious. Later we heard that two nuns had been identified as definitely non-British non-females. The nun scare had begun. The children's father, as far as we were allowed to know, was on a troopship en route for Australia, and we felt we must take action. Hedge-hopping enemy planes shot at anything that moved if they got through defences, so we were told.

We all went to London to the Grosvenor House Hotel, and the remembrance of that trip is positively jewelled. Living in ill-informed countryside, we seemed in a doldrum of drab survival, the days plodding by, the nights jollied up by the remarkable Tommy Handley on Thursday's radio, and nightly the voice of Lord Haw-Haw, that never-to-be-forgotten drawl, announcing "Charmany calling". One *knew* so much of his news was false. "Charmany has bombed and annihilated the station at South-wold," he said. In fact it had been totally out of commission for over thirty years, but, like a well-told ghost story, it made your flesh creep nevertheless. Seeds of doubt show weed-like vigour.

The Grosvenor House ballroom was given over to little groups of Bostonian ladies, each at a table. We had all been living in mackintosh-coloured garments, some vague idea of camouflage I suppose, and felt vaguely disloyal wearing lipstick and bright colours in a world at war. These ladies looked like tropical birds. I can still remember the one who interviewed us — the quill on her hat matched her pen, and her bag, and her fingernails — it was like looking at a lit-up sweetie shop at night, and we had forgotten lit-up shops by then. She was a charmer. This group had crossed the Atlantic by very fast craft to dodge the U-Boats, which were not then attacking America, but on the other hand were not particularly discriminating, so these women knew what they were at and why, and no birds could have been less bird-brained. They were efficient and kind, asking good questions with great discretion. Some weeks later we heard 'our' children had been accepted, and shortly after, madly excited, they joined a contingent and sailed off, leaving two desolate females behind them. My sister also had to break the news to their returning father, but he was practical and pacific and took it well.

Their first letters were full of the lovely meals they had had on the boat (Cole Slaw was the great American mystery) and the innumerable things to do. They were also all briefed on their exact weight: the dear U.S. felt that we had been on the brink of starvation. They settled into a household with three children of their own age, were apparently very well cared for there, and our tactful young kept their emotional problems to themselves. Much went on in this tangled household of which we knew nothing at the time, but at least they were safe.

A few months later one of the evacuating ships was torpedoed, and many children were lost, although some survived after many days in small boats. It was a horrifying occurrence. There was no clear news from the open Atlantic, and we all waited with bated breath. It was a period of tremendous bravery, both of these children and their escorts.

My sister and I settled in to a long, cold winter. She had her permanent worry for her husband, with little communication. I didn't feel much more cheerful. In May the Government had started interning every person of foreign nationality, whether they had been born in the country or were newly arrived — immigrant, refugee, Italian ice-cream merchant, all were labelled enemy aliens, collected from their homes or places of work, even mental hospital patients, and herded into camps. There was a panic need for this, recognisable in many of us, but the variations of arrest were infinite. Some were herded into large chill buildings and given straw palliasses; others were treated with great courtesy by individual policemen. One scholarly medical involved in laboratory research for eight years previously was picked up outside Cambridge by the country copper, and they had a leisurely progress to headquarters, conversing with great fascination via several country pubs. This academic, now a professor here, who had left Germany in total disgust at its behaviour to its inhabitants, had sworn he

would never return, an oath he has kept despite pressing invitations, and he always remembers this day with this gentlemanly
constable as one of the highlights of British civilisation.

Into this mixed mass of polyglot humanity they confined my
beloved, removing him with no notice from the hospital where he
was working. After some days of chaos in the north, he landed in a
suburb of Liverpool with three thousand others, and they were
given some miles of barbed wire with which to enclose themselves.
This they meekly did. Communication to begin with was minimal,
and as Liverpool was later subjected to concentrated bombing
raids, waiting for news was not easy. The war hit the countryside
in a totally arhythmic fashion, and rumour proliferated. In Suffolk
we had a large regiment quartered near-by, and the village re-
frained from locking up its daughters, so evenings were sometimes
lively.

Most nights, the air-raid siren started; later we would hear
that peculiar coughing as a fleet of Dorniers crossed the coast and
made for the Midlands, which were under continual attack. A
couple of hours later a different cough returned, more separated
now as there were gaps in their ranks. Occasionally there would be
a distant grunt and shudder as a lone plane let off a bomb which
had sulked earlier. We stopped taking cover, which seemed point-
less in a wattle-and-daub house, and played remorseless games of
Ludo with all sorts of inset rules relating to the battlefield. It
became quite agitating, more so than the bangs.

By day we sometimes combed the coppices with backpacks,
collecting wood, like two crones in a Grimm's fairytale. Fuel was
scarce and erratic, and the house depended on the central fire and
smelly oil stoves. There were several nights of heavy attack on the
home towns of our sheltering regiment from the Midlands, and
fury and despair filled the air like a miasma. It was no more easy
for the soldiery to get news of their homes and those that lived
there than for the rest of us. Listening to their boots on the road,
you could guess what they were feeling — no need to look out of
the windows. My sister's husband came home on leave from his
troopship and loathed the sirens. He sat under the stairs while we
firmly went to bed. He preferred the safety of the seas pricked
with submarines.

One night we were both knitting when there was a terrific thud. Our chairs left the floor, complete with occupants, but our fingers went on automatically. Then, as we looked dispassionately at our hands, our fingers began trembling violently in secondary shock. The British answer was to make a cup of tea, which we did, to the sound of returning Dorniers an hour or two later and the All Clear.

At six the next morning the doorbell rang, and the customary pebble hit my window. In pouring rain stood Jack, our village policeman, saying that they had found an unexploded landmine lying some miles from the Chapel end of the village. They were immediately evacuating that half to the Church half, and Medicine and the Law must go together to where the defusers were going to work. There might be difficulties: the thud we had heard might change into a big bang.

A sodden dark morning is not the best time to collect one's wits, and I loaded a rucksack with dressings, bandages, morphine and a syringe, and a few odds and ends clutched at random. For some reason I felt rewarded at remembering safety pins. We set off through the downpour, meeting a trickle of the west end of the village moving east, and their fruity exchanges added unreality to the scene. Adversity had reduced religious disagreement, and all the Church chimneys started smoking, to boil the kettle for the Chapelmen. News had travelled by the agricultural labourers as they went to work.

Jack and I arrived at a very desolate piece of undrained farmland, becoming more waterlogged by the minute. There was a huddle of Royal Navy vans, whose occupants were stripping down to vests and underpants, as they suspected a magnetic fuse. A similar weapon had exploded for the first time on the Thames mud a week previously, where it had blown a huge crater. We had some difficulty arguing our way through, found a sodden haystack behind which to take cover, then crawled round to survey the field.

About one hundred yards off lay a long black sulky-looking cylinder, its nose comfortingly pointing in the other direction. The disposal squad was beginning to cluster round it, even colder in their undressed wetness than we were, but their total concentration must have kept them warm. Owing to the possibility of metal contacts proving dangerous, all watches, buttons, boot studs were left in the van, and the men squelched in rubbers. There is something extremely sinister about a large black cigar-shape with a doubtful reputation lying in an innocent meadow, and a herd of curious cows over the fence did not help. Not far from it lay a crumpled heap of what looked like a huge green collapsed umbrella. The rain poured remorselessly, and we grew wetter and wetter, while our empty stomachs rumbled like the cows'. I lay on top of the lumpy rucksack, which kept me marginally warmer, but longed for the luxury of the firm waterproof cape issued to the Law. We lay there for what seemed like hours, occasionally exchanging whispers, our insides clenched for action.

Eventually, about midday, the huddled white figures slowly stood up, clutching a piece of metal anatomy, and stretched joyously. The tension was over; we all felt so weak we could hardly stand, and then furiously hungry. Jack and I approached the Beast. It seemed about twelve feet long, and three in circumference. Cut off it was a thick parachute made of rich green silk, and an intricately plaited green rope. Jack was given the parachute and I got the rope, and we drove back through the clearing rain to spread the news to the village so that it could resume normal living again. This episode left a surprisingly pleasant scar, a scan of ecumenical tolerance. Bombs bonded the community, where religious disparity divided it.

Jack's wife made him pyjamas of the parachute, but they were so thick he could hardly lie down in them, and had seams in most peculiar places. We hadn't seen material like that for ages. The rope which I received later kept our garden door from banging for many years.

JIMMY

AT THE CROSSROADS

XIV   RUS IN RURE

Shortly after this Jack and I were called out to a 'terrible accident'. The roadman had heard a shriek of brakes, and found a car driven off the road, in which were an unconscious man with blood streaming down his front, an unconscious woman beside him, and a roaring, blood-soaked baby. He was convinced of the worst, but fortunately bicycled to Jack's gate. The baby's yells sounded so natural, we wiped it off and a local cottager comforted it to calm. The woman opened an eye, and quickly shut it again and collapsed, blanched, but the man suddenly sat up with a grunt, which produced more blood. When we had stopped this by pinching his nose hard, he explained that he had dodged a cow on the road. Evidently he had veered off, banged his face on the steering wheel and knocked himself dizzy. His nose had bled all over the baby, which so terrified his wife that she had fainted. We drove them all home intact and got a garage to rescue the car, which would still go, although the inside looked like an abbatoir.

Moral: see what will wash off, then worry.

A much worse mutual exercise was in a cottage where an unconscious girl lay on the floor with a wound in her neck. With terrifying casualness, loaded rook or rabbit rifles were to be found propped up in many a country corner. A small boy had taken one, pointed it at his sister, and pulled. She died before we could get her into hospital.

120

RUS IN RURE

The townee is trained to think of the country as a healthy place. True, the air is fresh, but that was about all. For water there was only the duckweed-covered pond, in a landscape of rare, slow streams and smothered ditches. Too much of the land belonged to gentlemen for sporting purposes in season, for which cover was needed, the farm houses were often magnificent but in great disrepair, and indoors there was little comfort. The tenants lived in grinding poverty, often on endlessly boiled greens, the odd egg that they found from wandering hens that were rarely shut in, and shop bread dipped in Oxo. The odd rabbit helped out in the stew. Only in the village could you sometimes smell bread baking. They used the old beehive-shaped ovens behind the fire which were filled with burning wood and then raked out, to bake the delectable slightly smoky loaves made from flour ground by the remaining windmills. Friday was baking day everywhere, a custom I retain, and I always walked through the village for the smell. Many kitchens kept an elm chest full of flour, with a little box in the corner where the yeast grew during the week, to be revived with sugar and sour milk. As well as the loaves, there was a supply of Suffolk rusks – scones bisected and rebaked.

Rural good health therefore was debatable. Lack of cash, education and thought accounted for most of it, and the country-folk one and all complained of 'narves'. "I have the narves again, doctor," was an opening gambit. Now, I suppose, one might blame vitamin shortage, and many of them could not afford to take up the rations that we were allowed. There were no fat farmers, and their wives were thin and anxious. They all used to come for a dark nostrum that everybody swore by; it did them no harm, they considered it did good, and it was useless to give lectures on how to cook cabbage. They knew you boiled it for two hours, so that you could suck it in, toothless. They'd rather have 'The Narve Tonic', a bottle they had to pay us for.

The farmer who had married the vicar's daughter knew all about 'narves': she was in a constant state, and needed reassurance on all occasions. He always led the way in by the cattleyard, asking medical opinion on a series of bright green cowpats, or the state of Bessie's gargett – the inflamed quarter of a cow's udder. His animals' failings and his wife's were apparently interchangeable and the cattle looked narvous, too.

His wife needed to have her remaining teeth removed; they were in a desperately septic condition, and only the promise that I would give her an anaesthetic would persuade her to go. We set off, got her into the dentist's chair, and I started giving nitrous oxide with one hand because she was desperately clinging to the other. A large mackintosh sheet was spread over her, and the technician obligingly held her other hand. The dentist asked if he could start, although we both registered frantic clutchings. Against our protests he got going, and did a dexterous job. She did not move at all, although the hand sqeezings continued. Once the teeth were out, the dentist then removed the sheet. Mrs B's hands were neatly folded on her lap, and the technician's right hand and my left were revealed, frantically encouraging each other to calm. The patient's narves were quite untroubled at this episode, though ours were a bit disturbed.

Despite basic health difficulties, the village survived well. Those who were used to static green water thrived on it and, to their great credit, when some of the London dockyard children were evacuated to the district and the locals were warned they must boil the water, they did so and no untoward colics resulted. Most of the children, though, were very frightened by the country, and went back to overcrowding and nightly blasting after a few nights away from Ma. Many had come from Plaistow, where my paternal uncle, 'dear Ernest' the monk of his mother's diaries, worked. They all seemed to know him and love him, and he remained there as steady as a rock until his death. Some of his trainees work in underprivileged Edinburgh.

Death could produce difficulties. One totally insanitary cottage housing a couple of limited intelligence with three stunted infants under four sent for the doctor and midwife, just as the wife was delivering herself, apparently to her surprise. We helped out a tiny creature that breathed, bawled, and was apparently healthy. Having made both parties comfortable and seen that there was some food in the house, we departed. A few hours later the husband came post haste as the baby had stopped breathing. Sure enough, she was blue, and cooling, and beyond any human attention. I had had doubts at the time as to how welcome this arrival was, and writing a death certificate raised a big question mark. It was late on Maundy Thursday. I rang up the County Pathologist who said that everything was shutting up for the Easter weekend, and left the issue to me.

Conscience dictated a post mortem so, in a minute back shed, I did what the book told us to do under the circumstances, removing pieces of lung to see if they sank, being unexpanded, or swam, having effectively functioned. The baby had breathed while we were in the house, but what had happened later? Some pieces swam, some sank; it was an open question. The only thing to be done was to replace, wrap the tiny corpse in a disinfectant-soaked cloth, and string it tightly in a cardboard box. This had to be suspended from a beam under the corrugated iron roof, as there were rats about. The family took this as a normal happening. I sent off my findings, and four days later, when England had emerged from its Easter torpor, the gravedigger buried the little parcel, a life that came and went without apparently disturbing its family. When I left the district six months later, the mother was again looking portly, though totally uninformative.

Years later I visited this awful cottage to find that, with its neighbours, it had been tarted up as a bijou residence for the reduced gentry, with leaded panes and a fake beamed porch. The sewage ditch had fortunately been covered and delivered to a septic tank. The post mortem shed had gone.

Another family with narves lost its old auntie. They said that she would have gone sooner if the doctor had been a man, as she had never let a man touch her. When I said the undertaker would give her great care, there were hysterics: he also did the laying out, and the district nurse was on holiday. I undertook the job. As soon as it was over, narves were forgotten, and they extracted a bottle of vintage nettle wine, to drink her on her way.

Natural vintages were numerous in the village. Dandelion, parsnip, parsley, and every form of fruit, and gin full of pricked sloes bubbled away in many a shed. In one cottage lived two old sisters. Nettie, the elder, was the active one, Georgina, the younger, was a vast monolith who neither spoke nor moved much, but they sat in their small dark room most of the day, usually with a bottle for company, peering through the geraniums.

A PICTURE OF HEALTH

The postman brought a vague message along with our letters that a medical presence was desired. Nettie sat by her bottle, but Georgina was immobile in her bed, looking like a fallen tombstone. The story was that she had taken a tumble and hurt her side. Examination could elicit no speech, but it never could, and Nettie was half-seas-over. A huge abdomen feeling like iron dough showed very slight bruising on the right side, but leaning on it brought no objection from its owner, and internal examination from the bottom end proved a blank. She breathed with the speed, intensity and sound of a contented cow, had no fever, and a pulse like a grandfather clock. Making soothing noises, I left her, recommending an egg for her tea when Nettie saw fit to climb the stairs.

Next morning the monolith still lay as before, but her right side seemed to be yellowish, and there was a slight crackling under my fingers. The bovine breathing, stare and pulse remained unchanged, but obviously something was happening. As Georgina was registered under the Mental Health Act, I got on to the authorities who came and took her to hospital. Nettie gave them a bottle of parsnip wine for the ambulance.

Three days later word came. Georgina had died, and the post mortem had revealed a ruptured appendix and peritonitis everywhere. This was an awful shock. Pondering the case did not help. If there are no symptoms whatever, what does one go on? Does lack of pain go with lack of wits? Does the body hibernate with the brain? Can this only be learned by experience? Apparently. Nettie still had a lot of bottles, and appeared to be consolable.

There were some stalwart women in the village, and they found great satisfaction in coming to First Aid classes. Once qualified, they were licensed to wear St John's navy blue, with badges on their hats. They now felt ready for the front line, and would be more capable of carrying stretchers than their spouses. They also wore the white gloves left over from their daughters' weddings.

"Does this make you feel more professional? " I asked.

"Yes, and you see it keeps our hands sterile," I was told.

The Women's Institute was a great pillar of the community, and my sister had to conduct its meetings. Some of their handwork was beautiful, if bizarre: Easter bonnets made of decorated fruit punnets, and wedding bouquets of vegetables. Finding a variety of speakers in scattered country with reduced petrol was difficult, so I had to step in on the spur of several moments. Warming up was always a problem, as they tended to chat, but there were two stages one reckoned on before gaining their attention: one when they eased their teeth out and put them in their laps, and two when they all began knitting. After that, all was clear until we sang 'Jerusalem'.

We had our eccentrics. The village softie was not very useful in fuction, but had a pawky side. He was leaning against the crossroads signposts, signless now, and a large car drove up and demanded to know where the road went. Jimmy regarded them as a farmer would look over new stock, shifted the straw in his mouth, and announced, "It don't go nowhere; it stays roight 'ere."

When he died, he left a chest-of-drawers packed with prizes he had won at village whist drives.

Another oddity was known as the Prince of Wales. Clad in a soft hat, a suit, an overcoat and gloves, he walked the lanes all day, winter and summer, as if he were on a city pavement, and then went home to a red villa where there was always an enormous fire, as his mother was the daughter of a coalman.

A vicar's widow lived near-by, on a very small pittance. However, she felt she had status, and acted with the hauteur of a Mrs Proudie. Owing to the miserable pensions paid then, she was in receipt of extra benefit, which had to be called for every week. A message came to the surgery asking if I would go and visit her. Her medical request was for a certificate that the money should be delivered to her, as, when she went to fetch it, she found she was standing next to the man who cleaned out the village night soil, and this was below her station. She possessed a rather useless daughter, and two sons who had been discharged from the Army as psychological misfits, and she was putting pressure on the local Bishop to enter them both for a crash course in ordination for the Church, which apparently she considered possible. The poor creature considered the village beneath her, and used to complain bitterly that she was not shown the deference due.

Much has been written about the oddity of the churchmen of these parts, and much must have been due to the extraordinary isolation of the area. East Anglia is a place of beautiful churches.

Some nestle, some stand like great ships beside a stream which once acted as a port, like Blythburgh with its benign wooden angels flying along its roof towards the people, their toes towards the chancel. Some have three-decker pulpits of great elegance, and a positive impression of the importance of The Word. All proclaim how rich and vigorous farming and social life once was: the Big Houses, many by then sheltering an indigent heritor in one corner, gazed across the overgrown parks with complacency, and beautiful farm-houses stood at the end of brambled tracks sagging now as the gable met the cow byre. I wish a Jane Austen had been about in the days of its richness, to regard goings on with a cool eye, although Robert Blythe's *Akenfield* describes it well. The lusty township of Blythburgh, deserted by the sea, was now a pocket-sized hamlet, and the splendours of the religious of Dunwich had been invaded by the ocean's pummelling, with only crumbs of masonry left to be seen. The local people said they heard underwater bells when the storms came.

Inland, the village churches among their elms and greening churchyards reaching to the lychgate, where men rested the coffin before its last journey, still stood, with the sagas of their distinguished dead on the walls. The congregations, though, were sketchy, the incumbents often aged and set. Even before the war came it was only the ancients or the lazy who would take on a village which regarded the newcomer as a foreigner for the first fifty years of residence. One beauty of a building I used to visit for the peace, and the gentle sun and shadows on its floor. You could regard the war as an historical incident there, instead of a bleak mantle of fog, smoking up everyone's life. Then, churches were open all day: no one dreamt of assaulting their candlesticks or the rattling poor-box.

I went back one Sunday, hoping for some more positive propping of the spirit, but the congregation was sparse. A bent verger, a soft-headed boy pumping a creaky organ where a gallant grey-haired lady was doing her faithful best, and a vicar in a stained lace-trimmed surplice, from whose mouth issued a totally inaudible mutter. At least we were spared singing 'Onward, Christian Soldiers': the five of us would not have provided much incentive.

When death came, the roadman would dig a grave, as war service

126

was changing the working scene, and the departed was put into it, a pretty straightforward business. The war went on, the village continued its life as the peasantry always has all over the world, the seasons and the crops marking history's clock for them.

XV   A CHILD IS BORN

The summer slowly waned. My sister was pregnant, a sign of hope for all of us. There had been little consolation from the internment camp where Jim was incarcerated, and it was difficult not to feel bitter. Several of his friends had been released earlier, but we had previously discovered that the Stevenson Exchange Scholarship German youths of 1938–39 whom we had mingled with, partied with, talked seriously with, and invited freely into our homes, had left a list behind them, ostensibly for their masters, but conveniently ready for anyone else. This gave details of all their countrymen they could meet. Jim, having a Jewish mother, and being apparently successfully set for a life outside Nazi jurisdiction, had apparently been given an extra black mark, a gesture of spite. His three sisters and younger brother had all come to our country under differing auspices. The brother was now planting tea in Nyasaland. They had done their utmost to point out to their many British friends the virus in their country, but we were all prepared to be comfortable in our beliefs, just as I had been in Berlin. The three sisters were training in this country, as a photographer, a teacher and a nurse. One was interned, the other two confined entirely to their districts of residence.

Internment camp life was extraordinary. The greatest conglomeration of brilliance of intellect and artistry, intrigue, vice and thuggery, were all packed together in a drab Liverpool housing scheme within their thin barbed-wire boundary. The Camp

A CHILD IS BORN

Commander was a remarkable man. Recalled to the Pioneer Corps following early experience in an earlier war, he never forgot mankind was individual. In this he was helped by Frank Dwelly, the Dean of Liverpool's Anglican Cathedral, the only building known in Britain not used for war purposes that continued construction all through hostilities. At night the Dean padded about on the intricate roof, putting out fire bombs in the many raids; by day he collected every book he could find and brought them down to the internment camp, a smuggler's job as it was all unofficial. He even got a piano for a duo who heard each other play by chance, and who later became the famous combination Rawicz and Landauer. Professors gave classes and seminars, occupation of every sort was set up with minimum material and this unique group, a large number of whom were their new country's most loyal subjects as she had given them haven when their own had given them despair, occupied themselves with working for her as their sign of a future. When the raids on Germany started they, sombrely, found hope while the intrinsic Nazis threatened retaliation: it was an identifiable divide, which showed up the two groups as no questioning could.

A small group formed to whom English was a naturally used language and understanding its natives — a far more difficult proposition — was not a closed book. These acted as an advisory board for the masses, which was an essential help for the Commander. Neither he nor his juniors had any knowledge of German. The liaison group were all medical men.

Weekly letters were allowed, single sheets of grey, thick, shiny paper folded into three, and stuck up only after the censor had read them. Writing on their shiny surfaces had to make an impression, they could not receive anything else, so illicit information could not be got out by secret writing. For some awful yawning weeks letters ceased and then resumed. It turned out that their manufacture was the invention of one of the men who was interned in a second wave. The government took fright, having released some very doubtful persons, and therefore no more letters were made. This lack of news made such an awful hole in morale to those who depended on them that he was sensibly released again, a man who did more for all of us hangers-on than many a political Briton.

Others have written from inside the wire, and few of the more intelligent have cursed it, in its necessity. Many, however, criticised the distinctions made in those who were early enclosed, for many smooth and charming operators who had made a cosy niche in Home Counties society were left free, conducting double lives until some gave themselves away. Ribbentrop had decorated many drawing-rooms, had established himself as a charming fella, and had many copyists, just as devious. What I would like to record is personal kindnesses. One morning in surgery the phone rang. The Camp Commander had just been talking to his committee, one of whom had said regretfully that he could not write for my birthday. The Camp Commander took it upon himself to ring up, to send me his prisoner's love, and offer his own personal congratulations. It was my twenty-ninth; we had been deeply in love for six years, and this really was a rainbow.

The camp was supported by visits from some brave and shining characters. Early on, Eleanor Rathbone, a totally intrepid and humane woman, whose family had long been pillars of Liverpool, went to the camp, stood on a table among three thousand bewildered, despairing and often enraged men, and talked to them as individuals, an act no Minister would dare to do. Another staunch supporter of mankind was George Bell, Bishop of Chichester. Little of this ever reached the papers, but they were some of the acts of greatest personal civilian courage and intelligence in the early days of the war, and saved for our country many of the finest brains who have later blessed it. They kept them in hope. Subsequent accounts, written up or given by word of mouth, have been memorable in their understatements of obstinacy, idiocy, or sheer raw fear of many Government personnel at these times. One is thankful that the country received so many wise and experienced men as a gift, due to the European policies of the thirties. Many have changed their names and are now indistinguishable; many have been honoured in their own professions; many bear their experiences proudly, and are mildly astonished that these are as little noticed now as they were then. Forgetting is easier than remembering. 1940 was a year to ponder.

Work went on, in a blind daze. The sun shone with brilliance, the historical horizon grew steadily darker, and emotions did nothing to help digestion. The village plodded on, enlarged by the Midland regiment camped in its vicinity. One day I had done a round of about fifteen miles on a bicycle, with the black bag on the back, beginning in a tiny cottage where a child had pneumonia. No antibiotics were yet available for civilian life, so she just had to sweat it out in a bed shared by the parents. As I rode back I suddenly saw that my engagement ring, a crossed diamond and ruby, had lost its diamond, which had been smuggled out of Germany in Jim's hockey stick, waiting for a future. This seemed a ghastly omen. Wearily remounting, I retraced the lanes, leaping off every time light was reflected from the road, to find yet another fragment of quartz blinking there. Worrying about the child, I called back at the cottage. She was breathing more easily, and, full of my own trouble, I told the mother what I had been doing. She told me her other children had been playing with "summat shiny", which she had put on the dresser.

There in a saucer, in a sticky teaspoon for the child's medicine bottle, lay my diamond. It was like the story of the girl who found the pearl in a fish's stomach; I could hardly stop embracing her. She had little consciousness of my joy, but was pleased her small daughter was "not so 'ot, Lidy-doctor". So was I. As I mounted the bike and sailed down the final hill in a rainstorm, an enormous rainbow arched the valley, one end illuminating the village. Celebrating my luck, I thought.

Too true, it was. In those black days, the G.P.O. still sent Greetings Telegrams, graced by a gold envelope. On the surgery desk lay one addressed to me, its gilding keeping it intact, as the customary pink might have spelt disaster which my sister would have monitored. Its words were few.

"Jim safe. At home here. Love Mother."

Jim was our code word. Never have I loved a syllable more; and I never envied anyone else who found such a rainbow's end.

That was the most golden weekend of my life. By Heaven's grace, the dear old man whom I had relieved early in the year was prepared to come back at short notice to the practice for a week-end when no maternity cases or predictable emergencies were pending, and I tore off through blacked-out, bomb-torn London, and emerged at Waverley Station in the early morning to breathe deeply the clear northern air. Reaching home before anyone else was awake, I had the infinite pleasure of waking them all. We were all speechless, owing to innumerable unreportable experiences, and it all passed in a dream. But of one thing the recent internee was certain: the national situation was highly dangerous and, if we were ever to be married, it had better be as soon as workable. Owing to inept releases, he felt re-internment was very likely. As I had promised my sister a year, this was not instantly feasible, but the practice where he had worked before as a student in Edinburgh was still open to him, as the incumbent was due for call-up. A large rota of his previous patients, few educated in politics but intensely warm-hearted, had appealed earlier to the Home Office to release him back to them. Many of them had husbands, sons and daughters already called up and were were well aware of his early history; but they trusted him, and these factors were irrelevant. The Home Office took no notice, but we did, and their action of loyalty has always been a steady candlelight.

With all this buzzing in my head and consumed with impatience, I took the night train back to London. It went slower and slower, and eventually came to a stop in a totally blackened area still covered by night. The guard came along the train saying that King's Cross had been bombed, we were somewhere called Stratford East, and they would bring buses to take us to base. That morning was memorable. Day came to a smoking city, glittering with broken glass and piled high with great chunks of rubble. From the mouth of a tube station, looking as neat as ninepence, young women poured out on their way to work, their hair set, their faces pink, their clothes dapper and their shoes clean. They had spent all night and many previous nights on the underground station platforms, on wire bunks if they were lucky, but up they came into a crumbling world, putting on a willing face to share the mess with everybody else. There are times when acknowledging the human race is not encouraging, but this wasn't one of them. My inner despair lifted against real trouble, and disappeared with the night airs.

The day following return to work, the most dramatic maternity case occurred. A small, slim, white woman in an isolated cottage,

132

who had actually registered her pregnancy some months before, was brought to bed. She had never been much of an eater, but her good man grew good vegetables, and she appeared to have sustained her budding future on lettuce and tomatoes. The midwife and I moved in, and stayed for ten hours. After long and arduous effort, this small person — almost 'the tumour with the woman' we had been taught about in our obstetric classes — gave birth to an enormous son, weighing nearly eleven pounds. Babies usually appear well-greased. Nature provides an emollient with the dramatic name of vernix caseosa, which oils the womb's occupant like a Channel swimmer so that it may slip out more easily, helped by the breaking waters. A 'dry labour' is therefore to be dreaded. Mrs Crisp's waters had broken long before, and we had an anxious time, but when the arrival actually occurred the infant slid out in startling fashion. He was as thickly coated in vernix as if he were larded, and was in the rudest of health. In due course his birth was followed by a colossal afterbirth. This we gave to the husband in its newspaper wrappings and suggested it would enrich his garden, where he dug it in at one end of the runner beans. He reported afterwards that the fruit of these vines had won a prize at the local show, and further pods had provided a sensational altarpiece at the Harvest Festival. All went well with the mother, who was remarkably undamaged by her effort and fed her baby with great efficiency.

The mystery remains. How can a woman, eating with a mouse's appetite a mainly vegetarian diet, produce an enormous son with an additional coating of fat? Will the eternally changing cycle of medical advice recommend, in due course, lettuce and tomato as the ideal antenatal diet? All the village women had a strong belief in raspberry leaf tea as an aid to labour. Years later drugs extracted from this source had a clinical antenatal vogue, so medicine sometimes catches up with foreknowledge.

The year wore on, with increasing reports of impending foreign invasion. My brother-in-law came home on compassionate leave to visit his pregnant wife, by then well on in her forties. He left us with some ammunition to bedevil the enemy. Beer bottles were filled with some home-made incendiary fluid he concocted in the dispensary, and an explosive device fixed in empty insulin ampoules fitted in the neck. He guaranteed that they could cause damage when flung.

These terrified us, and when he left we ranged them along a shelf in the cellar, where some toads lived, reckoning we would reach for them in cold blood rather than in hot. Being more simplistic, I ordered four pounds of Epsom salts to sit on the shelf. If the enemy came, we could give him some strong tea, as expected in Britain, and lace it well. We considered he would pass on, having drunk it, and the effects would hit him elsewhere. Things were getting tight. Every time we heard a motorbike, we peered round the corner to see what sort of head-gear was being worn — tin hat or Wehrmacht helmet?

The village kept watch on the skies, against parachutists. We heard wild tales of disguises, — nuns even appeared again in these rumours, with folding motorbikes under their skirts. Saturday afternoons were my spell of duty, and I can still smell the floury dust of the windmill on the hill where we sat peering out of the square hole under the axle on which the great arms turned, into the darkening skies. Was that cloud natural, or artificial? Was that sudden flock of birds making its evening swirls, or was it being disturbed? Slowly the countryside would disappear into the mirk, never a blink of light to show where farm or hamlet stood. These years of lightlessness were the gloomiest part of war; 'Let there be light' seemed a future we could hardly believe in again.

When darkness fell, we left for supper. The job henceforward was the Army's, with its searchlights and batteries. These could be seen wheeling over the horizon, and we heard the chatter of the anti-aircraft guns as they acted on their spotting. It was only long afterwards that we realised we had been told nothing of what we were to *do* if we saw a nun on a parachute. Ride your bike down the hill and tell the Regiment? Ring up Jack the policeman, who might be at his tea? The real south of England was better trained in its instruction, and we were fed one horrific tale of an old country lady who had seized her hayfork and run through a helpless enemy parachutist who had landed, transfixed, straddling a hawthorn hedge.

That Christmas, 1940, was especially ominous, dark, gloomy and dank, the cats' ice freezing into skids under bicycle wheels as petrol grew less. Hardly any news filtered through from the brother-in-law, who was thought to be in Africa, and only snippets from the children in Boston, usually material facts about height and weight. Occasionally a box of candy would be sent by American well-wishers, but it tasted so oversweet to us, with our changed diets, that we used it for flavouring.

The village women decided to give the regiment a real Christmas dinner, and they stretched themselves from their reduced larders, stripped the allotments of Brussels sprouts, and killed their favourite turkeys. We had a huge cook-up in the village hall, and fed the troops. They were in a deeply anxious state, owing to recent heavy raids on their home towns, and this may have accounted for reduced appetites, but I can clearly remember how appalled we were at the wastage. We all shared out the picked-at turkey legs, and took them home for soup, and there was a lot of surreptitious tasting of left-overs. The local pigs had a marvellous Boxing dinner, and you could smell turkey stock all along the village street for weeks.

In January, one chill and early morning, my sister came along to my room to say that her pains had started. Still in bed, I had a violent attack of jelly knees. "Cheer up," she said, "I don't know any statistics on the moribidity of aunts," and on the strength of this I got up. By great good fortune a friend from nursing days who had completed her midwifery training had come up from London to see us through, and we proceeded with normality. But let no one believe that a patient and a beloved sibling are the same thing. The latter calls for an extra dose of adrenalin.

The baby came on apace, and by the time the doctor arrived, the midwife had delivered him, with my shaky hand at the anaesthetic. He was a lovely blond child, cried lustily, and gave us all great joy. I telegraphed his father's Army unit and went into town to register him. Only on my return was it noticed that Somerset House in due course would have an ADRAIN on its books, not an Adrian. However, it doesn't seem to have affected his career.

The next few months whizzed by; I was obsessed with personal matters. By mid-March my year would be completed, and, with a reducing practice, the old doctor felt like returning again. Marriage was planned for April.

The Dean of Liverpool, who had done so much for internees, had become a postal friend. I had knitted a thick jersey to preserve him for fire-watching nights, and he retorted by saying that he would like to marry us in his Cathedral. Such a gesture was overwhelming, but impossible to accept. My father was in hospital again with depression, my mother growing older under various cares. She had already been torn in two between a husband who persisted in seeing the depressed worst in our future, and a potential son-in-law she deeply loved, and whose entire family she had welcomed at various times.

We decided on asking permission for a wedding at Rosslyn Chapel outside Edinburgh, a tiny and beautiful five hundred year old building on the edge of a spectacular gorge. It seemed to fit our contrasts and our mutual delights. When this was explained to him, our friend the Dean said, "Well, may I come up and marry you there? " And he did.

This remarkable man had friends at every level, everywhere; he had consuming curiosity, sense, and a certain cunning when dealing with inflexibilities. In later years, if there was a strike in Liverpool City, he would talk to the unions concerned, and have an enormous service of sympathy, full of colour, music, grandeur and processions of all parties in that huge central space in the Cathedral. At the end, all sides would be so astounded by their mutual experiences that they would begin to talk them out. A long time later, we received a telegram: "Please send thirty thistles for St Andrew's Day. Won't the choir have fun. Stop"

He came up to Edinburgh and stayed in the Caledonian Hotel, where a queue immediately formed of waiters and other staff who had done their training in Liverpool's Adelphi, and who welcomed him as a delightful friend. This extended to all his guests, and the night before our big day, at last I met him for the first time. He was a superb host. Present were the incumbent of Rosslyn, who had been infinitely helpful, and Colin Dunlop, of Edinburgh's St Mary's Cathedral, who was just about to become a Suffragan Bishop elsewhere. He was so entranced by the whole proceeding and the story leading up to it that he asked, "May I come to the service too? "

A CHILD IS BORN

Next day good fortune nearly fled. In the morning I laddered my last pair of rationed stockings. The groom had to rush up town with his coupons, and we bought two new pairs for emergencies.

We all reached the Chapel and lined up. Our three ecclesiastics outshone each other; each had dug out the most magnificent cope he could find to gladden a wartime wedding, and we processed in behind a scene of episcopal splendour, in a setting that deserved it. As we entered, the sirens wailed loudly — there was an ammunition factory in the gorge below.

The organist played Bach's "Sheep may safely graze." Whether it was the siren, or stuck pages, they grazed for about ten minutes as the organist enjoyed himself, which rather upset some of our Presbyterian guests, but eventually we were well and truly wed. As we came out of the door, the sirens sounded All Clear. On the way home, which seemed the place to receive people best, we went to see my father in his nursing-home room. The poor man was really pleased, despite a further flood of dire prophecies, and we left him with my bouquet of gentians.

Up to April, 1941, it had been a long seven years.

XVI   STRANGER ON THE SHORE

Immediately after our wedding we went straight to our new home, an attic flat in the house where my husband had lived in digs. They had been gaslit, and the price of entry was the electrification of the whole building.

It had a long room with a wonderful view looking north over the wide River Forth, full of sky, water, and hills. We cooked at one end, ate at the other, and mooned over the outlook in the middle. The winter sun came in at a southern skylight over the cooker. A sitting-room looked east over a small harbour formerly devoted to fishing, minor cargoes, and a ferry called The Willie Muir, which took passengers over the Firth to Burntisland. His solemn three honks as he backed out of the harbour rang in the ears, as did the tones of the two foghorns, one a tetchy soprano, the other a rich bass which we christened after two of our former tutors whose voices corresponded. From this harbour too we had formerly had splendid expeditions with the University Sailing Club. These days were now over, and whatever activity was going on was supposedly secret, so one did not look at it. The three wise monkeys set the pattern for all of us who were sensible.

We had a tiny bedroom looking west, with a door on to a minute balcony, hitched open by my souvenir rope from the land mine. The bath, pushed under an attic roof, had to be entered crab-like, and the back of our lavatory door was decorated with all our wedding telegrams. They offered sixteen different spellings of

138

our name, which led to its prolonged occupation by visitors. As the proprietors of the receiving post office were also practice patients, this offered them great interest, and it caused a variety of address for many years afterwards. Any other country would have considered us as undercover agents.

We had a week for marrying, and getting used to it. We had had to find a locum and had little money, so we plunged straight into wartime practice.

The district consisted largely of non-planning; ugly grey concrete blocks had been plonked down on what had been beautiful seaside fields. Ten years earlier I had ridden all over them on a horse called Red Shadow, who used to prick his ears when he smelled the sea and go wild once he reached the Cramond sands, tricky then as now with patches of quicksand, which he dealt with by inborn horse-sense, but which were worrying nevertheless. Now the dead hand of civic enlargement had grown over it in a grey rash, dwellings, church buildings, a pub, a cinema, a few places to work in. There was very little public transport, and the minimum of shops. The new inhabitants purchased their food from philanthropic cowboys who had bought old buses, stocked them up, and thus made handsome profits from the lack of competition. The mothers had to push their prams and walk their toddlers to exhaustion point.

Having married an alien, I became one also.

It is a very strange experience. Having grown up in a stable society with very formal guidelines, suddenly to discover you are a bureaucratic outsider is to feel like a man without trousers. The fact that many people are unaware whether these are on or off does not add to your personal security.

A visit to the police was necessary. They had an office collectively dealing with Dogs, Firearms, Dangerous Drugs, and Aliens. There was an intimidating official there whom we called Dead-Eye Dick. His eyes looked two ways at once, he had a small bristling moustache, and he was totally po-faced. He had an unpleasant job to do, so this was unsurprising, but for some reason I felt he might understand my position. However, in his eyes, I was the black sheep of the national flock.

Geographical licence did not extend beyond the bounds of

A PICTURE OF HEALTH

Edinburgh without permission, and reporting at intervals was necessary for both of us. This state lasted for about eight months, and then, with references, I had to apply for renaturalisation. This consisted in taking a certificate from Dead-Eye to the City Chambers. Here a lackey found a Justice of the Peace, a small tobacco-scattered Councillor who was reading his *Scotsman* in a passage, and not eager to stop. With right hand raised, I affirmed my loyalty to King and Country, and paid £10 down. Feeling as if I had bribed the Customs Officer and had been marked with his chalk, I bounced back to my companions in Dangerous Drugs and Firearms to tell them I was leaving them for ever. "On the contrary," said Dead-Eye, fixing me with his active eye like the muzzle of a gun, "Your files will follow you wherever you go." I wonder where they are now.

My husband remained an alien, considered 'desirable' only in that he was doing essential work then in very short supply. The fact that we were working by the coast and near factories made this a privilege, but involved considerable caution. We were told of a gentleman who approached a porter in the Waverley Station and asked information on trains to Fife. On receiving this, he tipped the man a penny. This caused such outrage that the porter told the stationmaster, and the donor was arrested on the train as it crossed the Forth Bridge, an undesirable alien, who had landed illicitly shortly before.

There were some factories near our home, and every morning as the hooter blew a swarm of women would emerge, their hair transfixed with curlers and covered with a scarf, overalls and old shoes showing beneath their coats. On Saturdays there was transformation. A bevy of beauties would appear brightly-garbed and eager-faced after the morning shift, and go into the town to find light relief.

The authorities started worrying about the consequences in the young workers, as behaviour used to be a lot more straightlaced than we see now, and I was asked to go and talk on sexual mores. Posters on venereal disease appeared.

"Is it all right and quite safe to kiss the chaps?" I was asked.

"Don't kiss anyone in the blackout unless you've seen him in a good light first," seemed the soundest reply. It was to be hoped that aesthetic sense would help out.

One of the most startling features to be seen in the neighbourhood was fathers pushing their own children in perambulators. Such family sights had been an unknown phenomenon: the man would never be seen with sons or daughters until they had grown into companions. Wartime made companions of us all.

Work for my husband was absolutely unremitting. Long morning surgeries, visits, and a ten-minute lunch. Afternoon surgeries, visits, evening surgeries, visits. Supper by about 8.30 with luck, and the phone would go again, several times, later in the evening. At night, we reckoned on five nights out of seven being disturbed, and we never knew which they would be.

Wherever we went, we had to carry our gas masks and, because we manned a First Aid Post, a tin hat. It was quite heavy, and I found it useful for carrying potatoes home from the local shop.

This Post was a tremendous club. The whole district was embroiled in it when not otherwise occupied in war effort, and it was busy with meetings, practices and lectures. It also sported a huge ping-pong table. Nights on, after practice, we spent in riotous play. This was often progressive round the table with eight or ten of us in action, our tin hats clashing in frenzy. A great spirit of bonhomie built up, and years later we would meet greying heads who remembered these times with nostalgia. It was a special time of bonding, trouble and hilarity in proportion. In crisis, these unions are invaluable, and one looks back to peaks of joy in a black area of grim news, a continuing scaffold humour. I'd met it on a personal level in the young men tied for years to iron frames in the orthopaedic hospital.

"Good morning, Reggie. Anything special this morning?"

"I got a bad 'ip. What's for breakfast?"

They had shared it with their hospital companions. Now we could share it with everybody.

One day, we received extra rations. A small parcel arrived addressed to Jim with postmarks from Canada, Australia and England on it. It had been sent on to every known internment camp after he had been discharged, and held sardines, some palely khaki chocolate, and a smuggled half-crown. It was eighteen months old.

141

A PICTURE OF HEALTH

The phone sat on my side of the bed. Sometimes a patient needed a friendly voice, and, if they could not see you, endless sagas ensued. Sometimes they had had a telegram with tragedy in it. The doctor and a pill were the first thoughts in a house full of grief, either alone or with a group of relatives clamouring that something should be done. Talking it out often saved a fruitless visit, while an exhausted man could collect strength for the next day. Putting on the kettle for the British panacea was better occupation than waiting for pills, and was a means to company; the neighbours were always ready as support. Stronger spirits were sharply rationed then, and rarely considered, unless smuggled.

An old medical man came in as help in the practice, but his eyes were useless for night driving, which in a blacked out and ill-planned area was no picnic. With civic fancy, roads were entitled Grove or Green, and were rarely labelled, so that with masked headlights you had to creep forward in a mixture of faith and memory, learning the number of lamp-post bases to each road. You then felt your way to the door with a shrouded torch, cast downwards. Any fluctuation of its direction and you were considered to be signalling The Enemy. Many of the residents seemed permanently on the move, and were vague about the names of the streets in which they lived, so searching for doubtful addresses in the blackout took time.

The area was very overcrowded, and many homes were housing grandparents who had either been bombed out elsewhere, or their caring relatives had been called up. Sons and daughters on leave from the Forces would come and go, so the known names changed frequently.

In the district, those who had little made the most of what they had got, and were the last to grumble. Lord Woolton's rationing had allotted everyone an adequate diet, most of it financially obtainable by regulated prices, in contrast to World War I. This made a much fitter populace. Children then had often been underclad, sometimes sewn in for the winter, ill-shod, often barefoot. The Police Boot Fund dealt with this latter problem in this war, the children were better covered and getting extra vitamins: orange juice and cod liver oil were issued free to those under five, and the pregnant. To show the physiological need, you

142

would sometimes see small boys swigging their oil from the bottle as they fetched it.

My husband remembered the post War I years in Germany, when the blackboard chalk disappeared from the schools. The children were eating it, a yearning for the calcium they were not getting in the absence of milk. His family had been greatly helped by a supply of toffees, and malt and cod liver oil from the British Society of Friends. Now, our meat and fat rations were small, but we could get some fish, and vegetables were obtainable. We had some spare coupons for luxuries such as pulses, dried eggs, and, if you saved enough of them, ham and syrup, with some special sweetie coupons each month. Boiled potatoes, and the ubiquitous chip if you had the fat to fry it with, kept the mothers going, while their protein went to the men and to their children.

I did some practice work, but it was unpaid, as there were no arrangements for extra help. We had patients then under the Poor Law, who were outside the Panel system — the insured workers and their dependants. The authorities would notify us that X was ill: we would go and find out the cause. Some of the discoveries of poverty, clinging to a corner with a heap of rags for a bed, were grim. You could find the occupant only by smell.

One attic flat in Stockbridge was memorable. A neighbour, neat as a pin, with a room full of a clean bed and glittering brasses, had not seen the old lady across the landing for several days, and got no reply to her knocks. She notified the fact. She was 'snoring' she said . She could hear through the door.

She led me into the room. There lay a wizened body, sterterous and unconscious. There was a scuttering as we entered, and a strong smell of urine, overridden by that of mice. They had been all round, and over the bed, whose poor occupant had lain untended for several days. The room was ice-cold, a morass of old clothes, newspapers and general debris, among which was a continuous rustling. The old lady was at death's door, fortunately unaware of it.

The hospitals were choked. I knew it was hopeless to try ringing round to them late at night. There was no Central Bed Bureau then: you had to apply to each source separately, waiting for ages until they were disengaged, and usually having an abrupt refusal as soon as you opened your mouth. This exercise took up more of the day than a whole surgery might, and, if there was an epidemic on, was hopeless.

What little could be done for the patient was done, and she was given an injection to help preserve unconsciousness; it was impossible to restore active life. I made her as comfortable and dry as I could, and the neighbour promised to look in, appalled by what she had found. The old hermit had evidently been unapproachable.

I went back early in the morning. Death had been quick, but so had the mice. They had already gnawed her knuckles to the bone. I went to register the death, and the treatment, told the registrar the awful condition the room was in, and that the landlord must be confronted. When I met the neighbour a few days later, she said that a few hours after the corpse had been taken away, a new family had moved in . . . . .

I visited a large lady who could not walk to the surgery. She seemed to be constructed from about four vast pillows attached to a bolster, and had a comfortable face with a wide and toothless beam embedded at the top of it. On her mantelshelf grinned her teeth, a double set. She said her brother-in-law, a joiner, had made them, but they were not very comfortable and she mashed most of her food with her gums. She cheerfully complained of breathlessness.

Looking at her structure, I was not surprised. She was propped up in a bed which swooped to the floor in the middle, as it had not been built for a giantess. I said I must examine her and, donning a stethoscope, started searching for a way in. It was astonishing to find she was in stockinette pyjamas. Pawing like a terrier at her middle, I eventually found some elastic deeply buried in the rolls which courtesy could call her waist. This was very difficult to extricate, as tyres of flesh had to be milked out to prevent its reburial.

Further up, I searched the pink and quivering map for a point where a heartbeat might be palpable. Her mammary apparatus resembled prize marrows in size and weight. I heaved the left side up by degrees to reveal the damp cavern below, and had just fixed the stethoscope in a hopeful position when my hand slipped, the marrow hit me on the head, and I found myself on the floor, looking at the dust corkscrews under the bed and watching the bending mattress oscillate wildly above as the patient laughed her head off. If the bed had become a casualty with this treatment, we would both have received severe injury, although doubtless the patient would have bounced.

Between us we resolved her condition as obesity, with all its secondary complications. She lived for many years afterwards, diets proving futile or fruitless, her spirits a light during desolate years. Real belly laughs were few, and she had a real belly to laugh with — the whole room shook with it.

XVII   OTHER STRANGERS

The practice grew, busier and busier, the night calls more and more frequent. In time of national desperation the sheer yearning for survival grows. Increased pregnancies, many unwanted, occurred, and there were several women in the district who helped out their worried sisters. Abortions were regarded with horror. We had graduated with minimal sex education, and with contraceptive information given by the grace of one far-sighted man, the Professor of Public Health. Obstetrics had never touched on this subject. The general population had nothing but what it could pick up, the chief amateur advice being to have a hot bath and jump off the kitchen table. Many women, comforting men before they went back to battle, found themselves in impossible situations, yet the general public still raised its hands in shock. Men always considered this the woman's responsibility; for them prevention of procreation was unmanly.

It was a piece of barely concealed knowledge that money could buy you out of this situation, but our patients lived on every penny they earned, and relied on their sisters' help, where knowledge of sterility was minimal. Some of the results were horrendous. The unsuccessful attempts at abortion, of which there were not a few, always seemed to call for help in the night watches, the abortionists naturally having vanished into the shades. Their penalties were heavy if caught, but they rarely were; there was a united conspiracy of silence.

OTHER STRANGERS

Sons and lovers, due to rejoin their regiments at midnight, would be seized by inexplicable pains at 11.55 p.m., and demanded a certificate. Otherwise they would be classed as AWOL and incur military retribution. One female rogue practised a very fine line in instruction on how to fake a fit. The pattern was recognised after a while, and a little knowledge of the patients and their character and background was a help in identification.

Tuberculosis was rampant. The whole population had met the infection in the growing up process, and most of us had developed resistance, but in many people this was shallow. Increased activity, as in factory work or war service, precipitated it, and the tell-tale signs followed: loss of weight, hectic flush, anxiety, breathlessness and cough. There were certain areas on the city map where, if you put red spots on the street plan, they made constellations like measles. The richest local cluster was round one tenement where my husband found the owner, an open T.B. case, making icecream in his kitchen and retailing it round the neighbourhood from a bicycle. The infection spread, like rings round a pond.

At this period we had no specific drugs to help: immobility and fresh air were still our only curative measure, and hospital beds were in short supply. These were infinitely depressing, too often providing terminal care for the young, rather than the old. The good food needed there was mass-cooked, not particularly palatable, and not tailored to various stages of illness. I saw cold dinner lying on the locker of one patient who was almost in extremis. There was a dreary town clinic in grim rooms in appropriately named Spittal Street, where patients were sent to have official identification of their sputum. They were then officially notified, but treatment might be long delayed, owing to pressures on hospital space. In the meantime, the patients' families did the best they could, attempting a sort of chilly isolation in crowded housing.

In 1940, Edinburgh had received the Poles. Their country had been overrun at the very beginning of the war and many of those who had escaped were directed to the south-east of Scotland.

To begin with, came the officers. They looked singularly dashing, with red hats and beautiful uniforms, topped with long

147

swirling cloaks. They strode along the pavements like kings among the peasantry, and their cloaks occasionally engulfed passers-by. They then waited till they were unfurled; coming from a feudal country, they considered this their due. Those of us with brass plates on our doors had difficulty in finding the relevant polish, tarnished brass being considered the lowest form of sluttishness. Someone gave us the tip that nail varnish would preserve the shine, but it turned out there was a shortage of that too, as these splendid officers also liked fine manicure.

They were followed by many serving men, who were cached all over the country. Fife filled with training parachutists, and the northern mountains trained ski fighters used eventually in the Norwegian counter-invasion. Ardent Catholics then as now, they used to march back from their fatigues singing their national songs, and finishing the day's work with Vespers in the street, led by their chaplains. It was a deeply moving sharing of two nations. The Scots, often so rigid about Popery, recognised this as the beating of a rebellious heart, and rebellion was dear to them.

Poland had been decimated: was this behind the survivors' randiness? Many young women fell to their bravery and charm in no uncertain fashion, and occasionally to problems when escaping wives followed them up, or the Forces moved elsewhere. We have many Polish names here now, and a very interesting genetic mixture has resulted, the Slav sense of drama, liveliness and endurance mixed with the Scottish sense of national quality, industry and obstinacy, and their progeny show brilliance in many ways. Many of the children appear high in prize lists, and their fathers have adapted to their lives here with thoroughness and style.

A year or two later Edinburgh became host to the Polish Medical School, and they were given their own hospital. This was just as well. Certain Polish ladies who had spread their favours went to our Maternity Departments asking for measures of relief. These were, not unnaturally at the time, refused, but a bed would be offered in a specific number of months. This caused consternation, as apparently at home they had had access to an unrevealed way out.

A special Ambassador, Sir Owen O'Malley, came up to

Edinburgh to deal with this vast influx, and, as we knew his wife, we heard some of their inside stories. Their Medical School flourished, being given every help by ours, and a true bond grew. Each side struck sparks off the other and they shared the same wit.

Scots take to any stranger but the English, of whom their memory is a long and bruised one. A cousin who came up as an R.A.F. rookie, sited in the country in bleak and windswept barracks, said that if he were a Pole he would be invited to every farm in the district; coming from Somerset, he did not qualify. His older brother, now a naturalised Canadian forester, was here supervising the chopping down of the Caledonian Forest for our urgent timber supplies. When he wasn't spending his weekend leaves in our long room, he had no trouble at all in being entertained. However, his fiancée in Toronto kept a long distance eye on him, knitted him beautiful khaki socks with baby-blue toes to prevent either of them wandering, and sent us delectable plum cake to entertain him with.

By 1942 I was pregnant.

For quite a while I had been giving anaesthetics, but eventually got so large that the theatre staff thought I might dream off in the middle of a case, so three weeks before the expected birth I settled down to a waiting schedule. Owing to clothes rationing which needed coupons, this was useful, as all baby garments had to be handsewn and knitted, except for the supply of exquisite little jackets and baby boots made by loving patients, which would have fitted a small doll.

The waiting extended for several weeks longer than bargained for. One early morning, after my husband had been out of bed for the fifth night running, I awoke to find the bed shaking like an earthquake. He was burning hot, his teeth were chattering, and all up his right arm was an angry mass of inflamed lymphatic vessels. He had had an infected cuticle, and scrubbing up for a confinement had proved an effective spreader.

Luckily we had a wonderful chemist in the district. On being rung up at home in the dark early morning, he opened his shop and came down at once with M & B 693, the first of the chemotherapeutic drugs, in short supply and on prescription only. He was followed by a medical friend with hospital connections, who got the patient into a hospital bed under supervision.

There was then the practice to think about. By great good fortune we found a new graduate who was free to come as a stop-gap locum. The prime snag was that we had finished our petrol allocation for the period and the new request had just been posted off. I rang up the appropriate office and received the stock reply about going through the usual channels. Our sob story of emergency cut no ice at all, so I embarked on a tram and went to beard the authorities in their den, preceded by my ample front.

Three girls in flowered overalls were doing clever things with matchbox covers, which they were then painting red, white and blue. Whatever their war work, I said I must see the boss, and they said he was out. I said that I would wait, overflowed on to two chairs and fixed them with a stony glare, breathing heavily. After half an hour of this, they all went into a little office at the back and a little man came out looking cross. I gave him my story, and he gave me the inevitable reply. So I said that my baby was three weeks overdue and that it was a pity for it to be born in this office, but the choice was his: an office delivery, or some petrol. Within minutes I could leave, clutching ten lovely coupons, and dashed back to meet the locum coming out from her surgery, preparing to walk to her visits.

My exhausted husband in hospital was a bit more peaceful. The awful rigors had stopped as the drugs began to work, but he was furious at having to stay in for several days. Show a doctor a hospital bed he actually has to occupy and he reaches explosion point, unless in coma. The hospital was very kind, but he did not take kindly to being washed and given tea in the early morning when the wards were blacked out and stuffy. This was followed by a dressing round with a trolley one of whose wheels stuck and rebelled audibly. They had a row of colostomies to examine, the atmosphere grew foetid, he grew restive, and signed himself out to freedom.

The long-boosted film of *Gone With the Wind* had just arrived, and we celebrated his second day of convalescence by going to see it. It went on and on, and my concentration started to go, until I suddenly realised that the plot seemed irrelevant to the luminous clock dial beside the screen. The seat seemed vaguely uncomfortable. Were those mutterings in the back regular, or weren't they? By the time of Scarlett O'Hara's dénouement, they were. We thankfully sped home to collect a bag which had been packed for days, and went up to a nursing-home. My husband decided to return to work: two should labour.

Delivery was not much fun. My morale took a severe knock at being greeted as an elderly primipara at thirty-one. In those days, mothers were delivered stranded on a sort of bicycle saddle, with stirrups for the feet, highly convenient for the deliverer, who could sit down to the job, but a hideous idea for the deliveree. I am sure a lot of older women's back pains dated back to this archaic method. Our district ladies had had their own beds with someone holding one leg while the rest of them had plenty to cling to, and I remember one in the labour ward, against Sister's protests, delivering herself determinedly on all fours. However, all this paled beside the joy of having our first son, and an obviously rich supply of sustenance for him. When his father arrived, I hauled the infant out of his cot, where he was comfortable, and held him in my arms to make a pretty picture of a proud parent. He was rightly furious and roared like an asthmatic bull.

During the first two days, when he was feeding, the air raid sirens wailed. I always remember seeing this little creature pause; his tiny fingers, clenched in hunger and beginning to relax into waving stars, clenched again, he stopped feeding and his pupils dilated to great size, the first sign of fear. After a minute or two, sucking recommenced with ardour, and a great flood of comfort went through us both, bonding with a vengeance.

We were on the fourth floor, and at night in case of air raids, all babies were taken down to the cellars. Some of the nurses were deeply angry, as evidently ladies from the south who desired to conceal their pregnancies were coming to the north away from the worst raids, giving birth and leaving the babies for adoption. We felt angry too: desertion in time of war had an ugly face. The nurses used to try to smuggle the babies in to their real mothers, so at least they could see what they were leaving, but the Sister, briefed in their histories, thwarted them. She was a beautiful calm oasis of a woman, Sister Deakin, who saw the whole picture, not a glimpse of one.

A PICTURE OF HEALTH

It was a blissful interlude, concentrating on being a cow, but our infant was a very hungry one, demanding topping up night and day. As nights were so often phone-interrupted also, sleep seemed always round the corner, and the tiredness hung round my eyelids the full twenty-four hours. I often wondered what the night callers thought of the loud sucking noises, as they usually seemed to ring at nocturnal feeding times, and I dreaded overlaying our baby. Fortunately we had a garden where the pram could be pushed to a far corner. Beyond earshot, the child rapidly learned to sleep under the impact of fresh winter air, came in rosy and ravenous, and contented himself with greater regularity.

Winter war babies were pale babies, and in hospital we had been taught to prescribe an iron mixture, called after the paediatrician who had sponsored it, who shall be nameless. Its use became de rigueur, and the mothers nodded their satisfaction as they carried off their bottles. Two different paediatricians had their October first born at the same time as ours, and therefore three bottles of this brew stood on three medical nursery shelves.

Early in 1943 the three fathers met and compared notes. Each remarked sadly that their infants had spat it out in a fury, and, what's more, it had formed iron mould stains on the spit marks on their rationed woollies, to the rage of their mothers who had discarded it. We learned from this of the docility and sense of the out-patient mother. She did not like to hurt doctor's feelings, took home her bottle, threw it away, and the baby made its own way in the world.

We inherited an old Highland terrier called Morag. She had spent her early years walking beside an old lady in her Bath chair, and took gladly to walking under a pram. These then were solid objects, which could hold two children and a hefty load of shopping, so were subjects of regard. Morag was a most comforting presence in time of war. When children were asleep and the radio blared tragedy, her nose would come seeking my inert hand as a communication with living matter, while her short legs stuck into the air like pegs.

One day I left eight bread rolls to rise and came back to find only three, beside them a distended black bolster looking sheepish nervously hiccupping and rolling her eyes. I took her down to the garden and gave her an enema of soapy water, which she patiently bore and then took off — the first example of jet propulsion that I had seen. Some time later she returned, a lot thinner and happier.

Once in her old age, I came upon her having a very reluctant affaire with a rather horrible local tyke. She instantly regretted this, and we forgot all about it until suddenly she appeared indubitably pregnant, although greatly advanced in years. When she started fussing with her bedding, I settled down on a mattress beside her, and she eventually produced an ugly black and white object, for which she went through her loyal instinctual rites, an elderly primipara if ever there was one. She then settled down firmly to sleep, as did I. On waking in the morning, I found the pup was suckling busily, but what was that dark mat his mother was lying on? Shifting her a little, we found a flat fur rug. She had had a second pup, and promptly laid her bulk on it, realising, I am sure, that one bastard in her old age was enough.

We called the survivor Ikey, as the son of Tykey: he was no charmer and went elsewhere. Morag died in the ripeness of years, and her loving shade seemed to haunt the kitchen for a long time, until sheer hard work blotted it out.

Back with the pram in the garden, I would push it slowly under the apple trees, frequently raided by small boys. Their mothers sometimes stood guard with *their* prams outside, which would prove useful receptacles. Next door was a factory, separated from us by a solid iron fence with a small hole in it. One day, as I was pram-rocking, a hairy hand appeared through it, feeling for an apple. I seized it and shook it warmly, and it shot back with high speed.

We started keeping hens. Rations allowed us one egg per person per week, so this was a great help, and we could claim an allowance of hen meal, which looked and smelled like insanitary sawdust. I had visions of having to make scones with it in a crisis, but the hens liked it mixed with potato peelings, and obliged womanfully. We raised several broods of chickens, but they always seemed to be cockerels. Aren't more boys supposed to be born in war time? However, fattened up on extra potato, they made lovingly received Christmas presents with a sprig of fir on their chests.

Living by the sea, we were blessed with a sense of space, which could not be found in what we saw and heard. It was difficult to see much farther than each day as it dawned. War news grew darker and darker and censorship left us guessing. Telegrams of disaster arrived for those we knew concerning their sons we knew also. We tended to seize each hour for what it held, and cherish its good fortune.

XVIII   HOUSEHOLDERS

During the year 1943, my father was permanently in hospital, in a state of deep depression. I went out to see him with our little son, now ten months old. In those days mental hospitals were under lock and key for the severely ill, and I shall never forget the experience of following a sort of turnkey through a series of wards, with this little golden boy crowing and glowing. Patients who were permanently bowed in inner despair looked up, and to my poor father, doubly bowed under contemplation of double world wars, his grandson brought a gleam of hope that he thought had vanished. Pneumonia, philosophically termed the Old Man's Friend, claimed him some months later, and I did not see him again.

When our son was fifteen months old, his sister was born, a rosy and contented child. An eldest has the disadvantage of an uncertain mother who is learning her craft; subsequent children are handled with more security and ease, and respond to it.

Since the war broke out and again immediately after release from internment, my husband had been applying to join the Forces. After medical qualification, he had applied for naturalisation, but owing to hostilities was still regarded an alien, and was so aware that Great Britain was giving him the chance to work out his gratitude for its acceptance of him in black times, that he overworked continually. By now, he had been a decade in this country. He hardly knew his children as he hardly sat down at

155

midday, and only saw them in hours of darkness when they were either sleeping or shouting. Then they had to be shushed, as by this time he was exhausted.

Suddenly, in 1944, his call-up papers for the Army arrived. For him, this was a welcome into the Establishment; for us, an attempt to share his satisfaction, as we found ourselves in the same position as so many families in the practice. He could not leave until he had found a locum strong enough to carry three-quarters of the load; the old man already there could do little beyond sitting in at surgeries, and very limited daylight driving. Spare medicals were very hard to find, and some were totally unsuitable. We saved our bacon ration to welcome another refugee off the night train for an interview, only to meet his embarrassed refusal of such a wartime breakfast treat, as he was a very kindly orthodox Jew. The hens obliged him with an egg, but he went back to Birmingham. The slightly known was better than the unknown. Eventually an Irishman turned up, and the future seemed to clear for the head of the family: it tended to fog for the rest of us.

One day in May, in his new khakis, he said goodbye. His son was one and a half, running eagerly everywhere, a vigorous activist exploring touch, sound, smell and language, eyes alight with curiosity and joy. His daughter, at three months, a pink plump little rose, smiled at everything in her pram.

It is not easy to see your man, usually totally in control of himself and others, weep over his children before you go off to see him leave. Having waved until the train had disappeared from Waverley Station, full of dark smoke and steam on a dripping grey day, I climbed to the open front of a tram where the rain was beating in and cried back at it all the way down the hill to the wet grey sea. That station visit, and the few following it at the end of service leaves, gave such a feeling of despair that it was years before I could go there again without a surge of indigestion. Forty years later it can still clench the stomach, as can the unexpected sound of a siren.

He went off to military training four years to the day after the military had interned him. Great Britain was recognising her assets.

HOUSEHOLDERS

Life's greatest good fortune is to have full hands; to be able to use them can drown a lot of useless conjecture. Its greatest obstruction is when the faceless official prevents you from getting on with it.

For some months the raw problem was lack of money. We had hardly any savings at all, and at that period it was considered beyond belief to touch them. They were in National Savings Certificates, and you felt that this was financing the nation in its hour of need — rather like supplying the missing frying-pan in the side of the *Punch* aeroplane.

Practice payments were directly diverted to the surgery, and there was delay in receiving those due from the Army. Other monies expected were held up, and banks did not give promissory notes at such a time of uncertainty. Although our bank manager acted as an honorary uncle, promises could not be made until it was known what they were based on. For our wedding we had bought some real linen sheets, which were now unobtainable. I managed to sell these to someone who was marrying off his daughter, and this provided us with food and rent for three weeks.

By great good fortune the University came to the rescue with two jobs for me, one temporary, the other continuing on and off for over twenty years. The first of the Transatlantic evacuees ready for undergraduate training were returning, and these all had to be medically examined. They were a marvellously fit and upstanding bunch in comparison with our own young who were shabbier, which showed in their morale. I shall never forget the elegance of the girls' underclothes, beautifully cut brassières and neat, cheerful briefs on well held figures. We seemed to have spent years in threadbare vests and greying breeks with spent elastic. These tiny visions seemed far more vital than world events.

One of the medical departments found it was short of laboratory demonstrators, and I started afternoon work there, stacking the children in a pram, pushing it to a tram stop, embarking the pram fore and the children aft, and decanting them at our destination. While I worked they spent two fruitful hours in one of the animal houses, napping or watching the white rats whose keeper, Willie, gave them care of the highest quality. This care he also extended to our young. We had a lab man called Henry,

157

whose growth was stunted due to an early T.B. spine. He shuttled to and fro for me, from lab to pram. When his cheerful face appeared at the same level as the children's they screamed with joy and he would bring me back good news while I bent over a student, trying to encourage him to extract a spot of blood to examine from his own thumb. When he couldn't get it, he would use mine, which bled readily, but I often felt rather punctured by the end of the afternoon. Henry's only external pleasure was the horses. Every week when he was paid he ventured half-a-crown in sixpences on his choice; he reckoned he would always even out by the end of the month. I hope he may walk straight-backed in the celestial fields, happy horses galloping around him, and the cheerful shouts of children near-by. He was a good friend.

By the time the children were fetched they were very damp indeed, and had to be re-upholstered before the journey home again, but the system worked and, by the time my salary was paid, Army pay was coming through. I could breathe again, but it was an unnerving period.

However, compared to so many, I had so much. Our growing children stayed healthy and hearty, unaware of a missing parent, and my job gave me the feeling of pulling some weight. It was the evenings that suddenly brought emptiness and gloom. The house was deadly quiet, except for toots from the harbour boats or the booming of the foghorns telling the hours, and you found you were listening, desperately. The news on the radio did not help much, although Morag's heavy breathing did.

It was continually amazing how well people stayed under emergency conditions. The sense of national bonding gave everyone a zest in living, provided they were not tired out; this was endorsed by the reduction in suicides — contrary to expectation. When the first of a series of victories in battle succeeded a series of defeats the doctors' waiting-rooms were emptier, and people walked with a spring in their step.

Our war in the north was a detached one, for we were no longer in the raided area. The industrial parts of the west of the country, where the Atlantic convoys gathered, received the rage of the enemy, as did the south of England and the Midlands. Listening to the horrors of others is a wearing process and deliberately dulls the mind if it does not destroy it. First-hand experience activates: second-hand, little can be done except to try and help with the splinters that come your way. Over this period a strange inner change pervaded Edinburgh. The inflexible conventions were giving way, unnecessary social restrictions previously considered essential were now recognised for what they were, and people had no time for them. If you had to conduct that sort of social life, you could not do it alone: some background of domestic help was needed, and it wasn't there any more.

Following the Poles came far more English than had been seen here before; the southerners had always appeared to regard the north as a farouche breeding ground of argument and wild ways, frequently snowbound. They took to weekending in Edinburgh to escape the bombs and broken glass and buildings in London and, as they usually came in summer, they were thunderstruck to discover the brilliant air, the staggering views of hill and sea from the ends of the streets, the apparent normality.

Princes Street had its first liberation of ladies walking its length ungloved, unhatted and sometimes even with bare legs. The indigenous matrons twittered at this informality, but slowly melted. It was no longer essential to wear a woollen twin-set, a felt hat and pearls, real or mock — a uniform which had proved as universal in the middle classes as woollen underclothes in winter. The shop windows began to expand, the waxen ladies in tweeds therein wore less than previously, and that more negligently.

This invasion of apparently casual, amused visitors, revelling in a city undisturbed by fire and night cries, gave the old Establishment a rare poke in its corsets, and made it a much more interesting place in which to be young and adventurous.

For those of us at home, when there was time to pause, we seemed poised in history. Any deep thought about what was happening in the lacerated desert outside was so appalling we dodged away from it, as if our hands had been caught on a hot stove. From the distance of years it seems a long, grey period pierced with irrelevances and quickenings of the heart. The explosions of joy when letters came were like sunbursts: a prolonged thundercloud when I did not know that my husband was having malaria and blackwater fever in East Africa and no news came, was employed in furious walking round the neighbourhood, pushing a heavy pram.

Odd highlights still gild memories. The children and I, deeply depressed during this period, went to visit a dear Orcadian couple, who were childless and always amused at the human scene.

Billy was one of the doctors at the First Aid Post. When at rest his hands curled on his knee. He had rowed so much as a youth in those wild northern seas round the islands that it had become a natural posture to hold the oars. His welcoming wife, Alice, had grown up on a little island off the mainland, her father a skipper who used to sail missionaries to Labrador. They had both dealt with every kind of tragedy and weather in that stormy sea during their childhood, and the world's behaviour merely seemed a variation. Billy would tell of his schoolboy friends who used to lose their lives collecting seabirds' eggs. A trio of brothers, tying together the Christmas scarves their granny had knitted, used them as a lowering rope, but the cliff edge sawed them through, and they all plunged into the sea. He told another grim tale of his youth. During summer holidays in Caithness early in the century, they always stayed at the McDonalds' tiny farm where there were two sons. The older a hydrocephalic, was known as 'the Loon'. One year he was not there.

"Where's the Loon? " asked the young Billy.

There was a pause. Then the farmer's wife explained, "He wasna' doing well. So Mr McDonald took him up to the moor, and he slew him . . . . ."

The day we called, a whole pound of Orkney butter had arrived, wrapped in a cabbage leaf, the impression of its veins still visible on the dewy creamy surface, and Alice had just baked bread in her Aga. We all sat down round the kitchen table and ate this basic beautiful food in a gastronomic ecstasy.

On another occasion a flock of peewits had settled overnight by the water, caught by dusk one evening. Next morning we saw them wheeling off, flirting with the air like giant sycamore seeds, before crossing the Forth. Two days later I heard this wild and wonderful cry again, and couldn't believe my ears. They had originally roosted beside a pile of old motor tyres, and could not possibly have chosen such a spot for pleasure. When I went outside, there wasn't a peewit to be seen, but up on a chimney pot was a solitary starling, aspiring to lapwing grandeur, copying their whoop of freedom.

Prices were rising, our landlady had to increase the rent, and carting two children up and down attic stairs became increasingly wearing. Elbows always caught as I inched through the door. Both of these joints grew increasingly painful and, when officially diagnosed as 'bi-lateral tennis elbow', it seemed the sourest of jokes.

The time seemed ripe to find a more permanent roof. I pushed the loaded pram for miles looking for possibilities, but the city was chock-a-block. A licence was necessary for the most modest repairs as there were few men to carry them out, and few houses in a reasonable state were saleable that weren't impossibly expensive.

By 1945 one lucky day in a quiet crescent, I found a house that had been used and misused as an Air Raid Warden's Post. We were no longer threatened by bombing raids and it stood empty, the wardens now checking on blackouts from the streets alone instead of standing by for fire-fighting and emergency. We were still all feeling our way in the dark, possibly with dimmed torches, but had got quite good at it, as we passed another wraith or a solid lamp-post in the blackness.

Inside, the house was piled high with dirty plaster dust from battered walls, mixed with soot that had slithered from the fire-places. The wardens hadn't bothered about housekeeping. Plumbing was primaeval, and partially blocked; the lighting, worn-out gas brackets that had long ceased to function. Over the door was a notice saying 'Headquarters Harry', and Harry's men had worked by torchlight behind closed and not very adequate shutters which obviously they had never opened. There was even a non-functioning telephone on a long string: they had knocked a hole between two walls so that they could pass it through in case of incapacitation.

I went up to argue about licences, and met the usual stone wall. However, medicals held a little clout in this, and after I had pointed out to an endless series of petty and pettier officials that a doctor could not practise from an unlit home with no source of hot water and blocked lavatories, they grudgingly gave a licence for £250. With help from the bank, the house was purchased as a non-functioning problem from the Civil Defence for a manageable sum. It seemed a monumental millstone at the time, but, in retrospect, was the snip of the century.

The rates were still high, and, I discovered from neighbours, higher than they should be for similar houses in good condition. Another journey up town to argue with authority, with the usual result, so I demanded the chief, accused him in the hearing of his overstaffed office of blackmailing the Services, and, to get rid of this monstrous woman, he said he would send down an assessor. I left the place undisturbed in all its original mess, he came, saw and smelt, and the rates were halved.

At times, fighting battles in uniform seemed preferable.

One great advantage of this aged and elegant house was that it had a path opposite opening into a lane behind a row of houses, in one of which my mother lived. She could pass through her garden gate and walk quietly to see us. Her sight had now deteriorated with glaucoma, and this safe way to come and visit her grandchildren was a delight to her for her remaining days.

She was full of private glee. Behind her house, in the playing-fields which it overlooked, were some rather splendid wych elms. A neighbour decided they were dangerous, although well away from her house, and demanded their removal. My mother found the men at it, and furiously commanded them to stop, or did she have to tie herself to 'her' tree? As it was tea break, they did, and she immediately rang up the City Chambers and got the Lord Provost, a far-seeing man of his time. He countermanded the order. She received a letter, commending her services 'to horti-culture and to sylviculture', and promising that flowering cherries would replace the amputated trees. They never did, but the wych elms are still there.

The beloved nannie of my youth had returned to her as a protector, and she welcomed the children over during the day while I scraped off up to seven layers of decaying wallpaper in the mornings and went up to the lab in the afternoons. A joiner came to take the backs off the shutters, which were too shrunk to keep light in and draughts out, and with these he built book-cases in the house and a house for the hens in the garden.

162

Incredible though it may seem, in 1945 the sum allowed us covered his services, the electrification of the house, total replumbing, the painting of the outside and the unreachable insides. The rest had to rely on my itinerant efforts.

The hall was very high, with a cupola, and the ceiling bulged down dangerously, so we asked a plasterer to render it safe. He was a most proper man, a Church elder, who lent tone to our crescent by arriving in a black overcoat and Homburg hat, changing discreetly in a back room. After he had erected scaffolding, I removed the children for the day and went to work. In the afternoon I came along to see progress and met a blackened man in a black and dusty coat and gritty Homburg, walking slowly home, profoundly depressed.

Apparently during its hundred and fifty years of life, our home had periodically had its chimneys cleaned. The sweeps, who needed to squeeze through a transom in the high bathroom ceiling to reach the chimneys, had simply left the soot from their activities lying in the attics, and the weight had caused the bulge. As soon as our spotless friend had attacked it, soot and plaster had poured down on to stairs and hall. When I went in at the front door the floor was ankle-deep in filthy crunch. It took me a week of hard work to clear. Then he returned and finished his job.

Walls were then distempered from the top of a ladder downwards, and paint applied over innumerable window frames, doors and skirtings. At night my overworked wrists twitched and constantly woke me up. Gloss paint was as sticky as thick treacle then.

Furnishing material was only obtainable with coupons, of which one received a minimum; officialdom inferred that if you said you needed to curtain four windows, you meant two. However, you could buy unlimited quantities of white surgical gauze, which let a soft filmy light into some rooms, but you could not use them after dark. It was considered indiscreet then to allow passers by to look into your interiors, although after early years in Oxford, where there were distracting ground floor visions of undergraduates working, drinking, playing flutes or hanging out of the window, I always thought this a deprivation.

In 1945, before we were ready to move house, the paralysing

news of Hiroshima and Nagasaki seared the world. For our generation, both then and now, this seemed beyond the ultimate edge of sanity, yet only later did the true meaning of what had been done sink in. At the time, cessation of hostilities in the east was a lodestar. Many of my husband's contemporaries had been shipped on to the Far East, but his recurrent malaria, as he moved up and down East Africa from Kenya to Somalia, precluded him from this. How thankful I was.

An Armistice was signed: VJ, Victory over Japan.

That night I shall always remember. Our flat down by the sea, which we were so shortly to leave, almost became the scene of revels. The harbour, former home of fishing vessels, had been one of many up and down the country preparing the extraordinary platforms looking like huge upturned tables, which were later towed south to act as the Mulberry Harbours when Europe was invaded. We knew they were something secret and averted our eyes, but on this evening the whole harbour exploded.

Every ship, boat, workplace, burst into full flood of sound: sirens, hooters, flares, shoutings — all made a glorious cacophony in the night. I opened the windows wide, as if letting in the New Year. The exciting row rolled on above the unstirring heads of our children, and dreams took shape of what the final end of the war might mean, and the reunions that would occur for so many waiting families and their fathers. Many of my friends had not seen their husbands in three or four years, and when eventually they came home it was as strangers, especially to the children, a fate I was to be spared.

It was sad to leave the physical centre of the practice, which gave a sense of belonging, but to move under your very own roof is one of the greatest satsifactions of family building. Fate can attack the walls, but you can bar your own door.

Our blacksmith cut us two spare doorkeys.

XIX   A FAMILY AND TWO GRANDMOTHERS

Life settled down to waiting again, the tidying up of the miseries of war still absorbing consciousness.

Our first Christmas at the new house was celebrated by the arrival of my husband's brother and sisters.

His brother had come to this country as a schoolboy of fifteen in 1937, an athletic and lively youth, of fixed indoctrinated ideas on the inadequacies of the U.K. He had suffered semi-isolation in schooling from the age of about ten due to the racial situation in Germany, and there had been effectively brainwashed as to the state of our decadence. This separateness had hardened his attitude which only softened a little when he was skiing alone, or floating down the Neckar alone in a canoe, occasionally with an umbrella as a sail. My husband had been at school at Salem, under the redoubtable Kurt Hahn. When his pupil's brother arrived in Britain, Hahn took him in to Gordonstoun where he had reconstructed his school. After two years there which were a very different sort of education, the boy had gone out just before the war to plant tea in Nyasaland (now Malawi), caught an undiagnosed virus later discovered to be poliomyelitis, and eventually been shipped home. I shall never forget opening the door three years later, expecting the familiar vast silhouette, and receiving a thin, limping, yellowed ghost, with diminished hand muscles. However, after a series of operations he was greatly improved physically, and went to work for his firm in London. Following his last spell in hospital there, under the influence of the buzz bombs and an admirable nurse to whom he had just got engaged, a new man emerged — lively, funny, eager to do things instead of theorising, and he brought his delightful girl to stay. Two of his sisters also arrived from their various occupations; the third was busy nursing. It was the first Christmas the children really woke up to, aged two and three, though I could still remember the wonder in the dilated eyes of our two-month-old firstborn, gazing at his first candlelit tree.

Christmas Eve has always been special in our family. The night before, the tree is decorated — white candles, red apples, golden oranges and silver angels' hair. Slowly the additions have increased: glass balls, straw stars, tiny figures, varying with the dimensions of the annual spruce — but always the real candles and the apples are there.

No-one could see it until the Eve, when the little silver bell was rung and the children came in, wide-eyed in anticipation, to meet Father Christmas who catechised them solemnly. For years they believed in him, until the day his beard slipped and showed Dad's dimples, but it has always started as a solemn occasion, and all generations approach the tree with respect. Carols are sung, and candle flames shine back from shining eyes. Real candles generate care: electricity you take for granted.

Years later their father brought home a spectacular Nativity, the stable in bog oak, the figures, starkly plain and primitive, in boxwood, carved by a patient, a sculptor who had been a shipwright. Joseph and Mary, the angels, the shepherds, the wise men, a donkey, and a dog stand wondering round the holy Child. The cow has lost her horns through being loved with clutching abandon, but continues her bovine regard.

My husband's family had not met as such since leaving their family home, and it was an emotional reunion for everyone, only the central figure missing.

His main Christmas present was his new doorkey, sent to a camp near Nairobi in inappropriate wrappings, but it was six months yet before he could come home to use it.

The Netherlands were slowly cleansing themselves of the slime of forcible occupation since the Nazis had burst their frontiers in 1940. There was a general appeal to take into our houses the Dutch youth who had especially suffered. We had not, as yet, heard of Anna Frank.

Seventeen-year-old Dik came to us, tall, thin, blanched, and very courteous. Some time before, an Allied bomb had hit his house in Amsterdam, incinerating his mother. At the time he, his brother and his father were all dodging from one house to another, to avoid conscription by the Germans. Latterly, their diet had often been tulip bulbs from neglected fields.

Slowly, he gained strength and morale, in what appeared to him a haven of peace, despite children's uproar. He had wanted to become a child psychologist, but life in close contact with infants of two and three took the gloss from this dream. One day, he asked in some desperation, "My dears, *must* you make that terrible noise? "

He went home after a month, resumed school, entered university, made an effective career as a business consultant, and is now the multilingual dean of an establishment of Dutch learning, with a grown-up family. He does not grudge our children compelling him to have second thoughts.

In 1946, in hot summer, the master returned.

The telegram from Africa arrived, and then came the wait while the ship felt its way back up the coast, through the Suez Canal, the Mediterranean, the Bay of Biscay and up the Channel — all those great geographical points now known only to merchant seamen. The anticipation that we used to know is now taken by the throat as people descend from the skies before their messages are delivered.

I went to London to greet a darkly-tanned almost-stranger, with a head-turning smile in the demob suit, shirt, shiny shoes and hat distributed by a grateful nation to its returning soldiery. The balloons were out of the sky now, the lights were on all over the place, the dark night heavens no longer criss-crossed with gold fingers searching for a tiny silver plane. The traffic sounded cheerful instead of dire, and, except for the dark piles of rubble already sprouting their explosions of field flowers under the brilliant towering fireweed, the heart of the city was beating strongly again. After the Plague and the Great Fire of three

A PICTURE OF HEALTH

hundred years before, perhaps the same spirit bloomed.

We came back to take the car off its wartime blocks, and to fetch the children, on a dazzling summer day. They were staying on a farm in the Borders with a beloved helper. The toddler and the rosy bundle my husband had wept over two years before rushed out into the sun, shining thistledown-headed, with browned limbs, first dumb and then shrieking with joy. I think children recognise their family smell before anything else.

We came back to a few days of exploring the owner's new premises and surroundings, the beginnings of the garden which had been Headquarters Harry's junk heap, but now held bantams in their back-of-the-shutters house, a large sandpit, and a double white cherry tree. Over the garden wall ran the Water of Leith, a source of continual bird life and pleasure, except when it overflowed.

Then it was back to furious work, after the depths and the heights. The return was celebrated a year later by the birth of a round little daughter, and another year later a son as her companion.

This held great poignancy. A month beforehand my mother, who at seventy-six was still playing the organ every Sunday, glaucomatous but gallant, slipped and broke her leg. She lay on her bedroom floor (shiny linoleum – no carpets for an older generation) until Nannie found her. She refused at first to ask me for help, since I was in 'an interesting condition', as the term then was, but eventually I was fetched and got her to hospital. Alas, she started failing; the last glimpse was of a barely-conscious silver-haired lady with tubes snaking in and out of her. Before she died she asked if her grandson had yet been born, and he was, a fortnight later, a bitter-sweet experience.

Her life had been one of wit, enormous strengths of acceptance, two world wars, desperation with a depressed husband, but she was always a support for four daughters, often against great difficulties. Her last six years had been easier, with grandchildren within reach, one of the greatest balms of old age, and our older pair could weep for her when I told them she was dead. The recent youngest used to sit in her arm, a rotund sphinx, her golden golliwog head mixing with a smooth silver one. A continuously

168

staunch background to us, she had plunged far deeper and lived far more penuriously than we had, yet, rich in human relationships, she was a prop to several generations and we missed her dreadfully. We had shared a feast of family jokes, and suddenly there was silence.

A year later we received my husband's mother.

Her husband had died in 1941, shortly after they had received news of our marriage by circuitous international routes via his Swiss academic pupils, many now professors themselves. Shortly after his death, the protective university umbrella removed and all her five children out of touch in enemy country, she was privately told in the academic milieu where she had lived for nearly forty years that she was about to be hounded, her father having been Jewish. In her sixties, therefore, this lady recently widowed, with no supportive family, packed a rucksack, left her house in the night and took to the woods, hills and the occasional doors of friends and neighbours in the southern frontiers of Austria and Germany, wherever she thought that the sojourn of a day or two would not cause trouble.

She carried no ration card; they were not issued to those who were supposed to wear the yellow star. Typically, she found most help from peasants who did not know her. With botanical training and experience of the hunger of the First World War, she knew every bush, berry, mushroom and toadstool that was edible, and the forests were full of them. In old clothes and a head kerchief framing her wise wrinkled face, she could pass for an unnoticed peasant woman. Several times, she was peeling potatoes in a cottage when the S.S. came. She became 'Tante Erna', a refugee from Hamburg deafened by gunfire and unable to hear what was said. A northern accent could be assumed in need, but, apparently dull of hearing, she was rarely asked to speak. By this device she was ignored.

With no news of her family, very rarely of friends, she wandered the countryside like an early pilgrim, with no aura of holiness to protect her, only hunger, and an incredible determination. When in 1944 she learnt that Mainz was in the hands of the Americans, she crept back one night to Heidelberg, was re-admitted by her faithful Marieken, maid of many years, who had filled the house with bombed-out lodgers to prevent its requisition, and took refuge in the cellar under a pile of feather beds, where for the last weeks of the war, she listened to the B.B.C. with eager ears. "Without Churchill's voice, I would have died there," she told us later.

When the American troops were sweeping up the Neckar valley, the retreating Nazis wanted to destroy the ancient Neckar Bridge in Heidelberg. She stiffened the population's resistance to this vandalism, and it was spared. When the Americans reached Heidelberg, she emerged, and when she could get a passport, came to us to see her grandchildren.

This visit was not of the happiest. After all the years of deprivation, she was ill with beri-beri, feeling deeply unwell but refusing bed-rest. She was always cold but terrified of our open fire after a lifetime with a great warm enclosed Kachelofen, and would sit in the furthest corner of the room, rubbing dry hands together and longing for endless talks with her son, who only appeared late at night and exhausted. Owing to perpetual hunger on the run, she had eaten when and where she could, usually a plethora of potatoes. She still demanded these in large quantities as they made her feel less alarmed about the next few hours, and this was not an ideal diet for an elderly lady. We were still severely rationed and, except for our blessed bantams, had little protein, not a dietary programme to build anyone up from deficiencies. The children were at the most demanding stage of the developing ego, and not loving little lapdogs. She decided she must go home to ways that she was used to, via a daughter by then married to a Norwegian.

At that time Norway was even less welcoming. They had been occupied by Germany, and their wounds were still open. I had recently been there, and walking the streets of Oslo you felt like a ghost. No-one met your eyes in case they were alien ones. The long green strip by the Castle still held bunches of flowers, renewed daily, to commemorate the daily quota of Norwegians who had been picked up at random and shot there. The cold was worse too, so eventually she went back to Heidelberg, and her fiercely loyal Marieken.

Here she plunged into work which she saw had to be done. The city swarmed with refugees, many widowed, and to these

she related. She started a headquarters in her house where they
came and sewed, making clothes for themselves or for sale, from
any material they could lay their hands on. The sale made money
for itself and the group grew, gaining in companionship and self-
respect.

Heidelberg became the headquarters for the U.S. forces. The
American women following up the troops, for ever on to prac-
ticalities, became interested in her work, and donated clothes,
time and encouragement. The American incursion was a very
successful one. They represented all the Germans admired: poise,
efficiency and self-confidence, and they had been well schooled in
manners. To watch them directing the traffic with a wave and a
smile, instead of the previous shaken fist and a whistle blast was
an education.

Their women were no idlers. They looked for the gaps where
they could help and used them with imagination. Some years
later when we were over there, I went with a group to an old
castle, packed with geriatric refugees from bombed cities. The
Americans had made a list of their birthdays, and each appointed
herself as a godmother to her Geburtstagkind, who shared her
birthday month. Each month they went there laden with a
splendid supper that everyone shared, and each 'Birthday Child'
received a small present and a personal bottle of wine. It was
unsophisticated, happy and charming, and far from any charitable
act. These wrinkled old faces responded to the warmth of their
hostesses — one man had tamed a squirrel which sat on his
shoulder and acted as a substitute child.

The American women told their officer husbands about my
mother-in-law and, with her excellent English, long experience and
obviously deep wisdom, she became a fount of knowledge and
intelligence for them, and a source of trust. She became a sane
representative, a standard for the city, was asked to its ceremonies,
and considered a necessity in international discussion.

A long time later, my husband and a friend were supervising the
order of a cake for her seventy-fifth birthday in one of the main
cafés. It was to have a map of the world on it, representing where
the family diaspora had finally landed them; two in the British
Isles, one in Canada, one in New Zealand, one in the United

States. A newspaper reporter overheard this and on the day of the birthday there was a major splash in the local press, two oompah bands came to play outside her house, and the downstairs rooms were ablaze with floral tributes. Touched deeply by the warmth of friends, she could hardly contain her contempt for a community that could turn its coat in such an overt manner after previously casting her out.

When Konrad Adenauer was President, he wanted to give her a medal, which she promptly refused. However, when he was succeeded by Willy Brandt, who humbly asked her to receive one, she accepted it. She respected its origins. The same year her older son had been honoured in Britain by the Queen, and she felt this a fitting rejoinder. He joined her and Marieken, who stood throughout a lengthy ceremony. Afterwards Marieken gave a graphic account, bursting into shrieks of laughter. *Her* mother, having given birth to ten children, had been sent one of Hitler's medals in token of glorious motherhood, and had immediately sent it back.

My implacable mother-in-law, having lived through so much grey desolation and horror, managed to travel to all the places on her birthday cake and more, visiting her children and the various conferences of the World Association of University Women. When the meetings were dull, she donned dark glasses and slept behind them. She also acquired a hearing-aid which she could switch off.

Having lost touch with her own children from their teens onwards, she became a very rewarding and, one hopes, rewarded grandmother to seventeen descendants, all of whom held her in deep respect and affection. They liked nothing better than her conversation, usually followed by a spell with Marieken (whose maiden name had aptly been Fröhlich). The kitchen resounded to their loud mirth, sometimes regarded jealously by their grandmother. Shrieks were not her métier. A gentle vibration and crinkling of her fascinating wrinkles was as good a response, and her wisdom was eighty years deep in experience and trial.

She lived until sudden death claimed her at ninety-five, in full possession of her many factulties, at last knowing she was rich in the love that she had had to forego years before.

172

THE FLOOD

XX   GROWING PAINS

When our youngest son was a month old, in the drenching August
of 1948, the river water rose and flooded us all.

Neighbours had kept a tame duck and had removed a stone in
their garden wall to let it out for a swim, but it had always preferred land life. Forty-eight hours of constant rain swirled the river
through the hole and the gardens of many of the neighbours,
including that of the duck's owners, (who had eventually eaten it
and were away on holiday), and we all had a backwash into our
houses. Warned overnight by the police, we had lifted movables on
to tables in the basement, and left candles to light if the electricity
failed. In the morning we heard a gentle clanking and, descending
the basement stairs, found an infant's potty like a gondola gently
rocking on the dark grey surge. We rescued all our candles and
some cold breakfast and paddled upstairs again for a picnic. We
also collected some refugees who had been washed out of the
basements where they lived along the road. When we came back
it was to find a candlelit floor. It happened to be my birthday,
and the children had considered this a specially arranged celebration.

It all caused a lot of smelly excitement, especially when they
brought home lavish accounts of the debris floating in other
people's areas. Ours still held the errant pot, which rotated slowly
until one of the firemen who came to pump us out sank it with
his giant boot. The house smelt dank for a long time, and years

173

afterwards in a dark cavern under the area stairs, we found the tin Army trunk, full of old flood water and rotted canvas objects. One of the interesting findings was that the hens, who on the day of the flood had retreated nervously to the highest perches in their house, descended and laid like mad. Perhaps the alluvial remains were full of rich plankton.

That summer flood rendered unsafe seven railway bridges between Edinburgh and Berwick, and destroyed a blanket mill.

Our sister-in-law was staying with us at that time, imminently expecting her first baby. To try and pass her tedious wait, she was taken for a drive round the sodden hills with our children. Our elder daughter, never very stable in cars, proceeded to be very sick all over her aunt, as, she stated, "Mummy said to be very careful of my new plastic mackingtosh." This experience, plus the excitement of splashing through bumpy hollows, accelerated matters, and they came back from the expedition just in time to pick up a pre-packed suitcase and deliver the now labouring mother into care, where she shortly gave birth to a vigorous daughter.

Just as this news came through, and the new father was due to come north, two huge Dutch youths with laden bicycles appeared at the door. They announced that someone had written to warn of their arrival, but in fact the letter did not appear until a week later. We put them up for some days, after a sortie to buy an enormous saucepan and an enormous frying-pan, as our numbers had swollen to ten. They then declared that they were vegetarians, so further ingenuity was called for. Once the surrounding country-side had dried up a bit, they passed on to explore the squelching Highlands. A mid-August to be remembered.

When the explanatory letter arrived, it was from the Dutch doctor called back to national service in 1939, to whose departure I had owed my first job. He had survived the war, heating himself and a budding family by tapping a source of electricity from the flat below him, then occupied by German forces. Later he had removed his sports car from beneath a pile of hay bales where it had been buried for six years, and by 1948 he was qualifying as a neurosurgeon in Amsterdam. He later visited us with his wife, and she bedazzled us with the first sight of nylon stockings, introduced by their occupying American forces.

The remorseless medical rhythm had returned, although we were insulated by living a bit further away from the practice centre. Patients still like to hear the doctor's voice, although out of hours, and occasionally one would peal the doorbell. We had several well-known cheerful bodies who loved the bottle and thought we would like a call when they were fu'. Every now and then one of the trawlermen would appear with a large damp package of fish to which I would endeavour to do justice. All the rest of the family insisted it was made of bones and black mackintosh.

The lot of these fishermen had improved immeasurably. In early years they had often been off work for weeks with painful salt water sores that would not heal. Chemotherapy had changed their lives by healing these quickly, and, instead of scraping a living that could desert them for long intervals, they were now becoming prosperous. One used to come off his boat directly to the surgery to ask my husband to lock up his earnings, some hundreds of pounds, until he had had his first pub visit. When sober, he'd reclaim the packet, and take it home to his wife. With odd mines still catching in their nets, and the sea an unpredictable mistress, their life was still dangerous, but less despairing.

When we were little, we used to go down to the sea past their cottages and admire the handknitted long-johns of pink and baby blue flapping on the washing-lines. Now that their clothes were becoming less dreadnought, and did not become so sodden, the men were dandies ashore, and living in wall-to-wall carpeted houses.

The advent of Nye Bevan's National Health Service in 1948 started to make a tremendous difference to the country's health problems. Instead of resignation in the face of illness, everyone developed hope again, but the medical personnel were not ready for the sudden swamping of resources. Understaffed surgeries with little space were filled to bursting now medicine could be afforded by all, and patients stood at the door in the rain waiting to get in. Often the doctor's wife would have to leave the stove to deal with incessant calls for visits, her baby on her arm, the phone ringing, the doorbell pealing. The Service was a superb conception, but general medicine paid a crippling price to start with. An

175

unpleasant system had developed, some doctors taking over shops as consulting-rooms that were manned for a few hours a day for what used to be described as the "Panel patients", while they visited and consulted with private clientele. This gave rise to the two-tier recriminiations we hear of still and sadly divided the medical ranks.

When the men had returned from the war, the young and eager wanted to embark on the medical specialities, and started scrambling for places, but the returning specialists, not surprisingly, had priority. General practice, the apparent alternative to years of specific training, welcomed the survivors with grinding and increasing exhaustion and irascibility. True, they no longer had to purchase the privilege of practice financially, but the pressures at that period were wearing. Much jealousy arose, and not a little chasing after openings.

On his return, my husband found many of his patients had changed to other doctors spared military service, as his substitute had never set out to please or to practise with much intelligence or knowledge of human frailty. These other doctors were not above referring to him as "that foreign doctor down the road, who would do them no good." If they rang up, I felt like acquiring a broken accent to please them, but kept as smooth as possible (for which one could hear occasional surprised responses).

We got bored by this behaviour and asked four of the most limited and occasionally virulent along to a good meal which, out of curiosity, they all accepted. This introduced civility into the proceedings, and rendered intercommunication a great deal easier. It taught me the immense curative power of Good Food. The blessed bantams had helped out again.

For the last years general medicine had limped along with ageing personnel who regrettably were often regarded with contempt rather than concern by their hospital brethren. The specialist tends to forget that his patient failures may frequently desert him, by death or despair. The general practitioner has to live with his failures unless they leave him by choice, propping up an inadequate tenement of the flesh, trying to maintain the spirit within enough to fight another day. This is one of the tragic medical divisions. The patient, who should prove the apex of the exercise, his care managed by a combination of talents, is often failed by inadequate communication between the parties concerned.

I remember in the war the wife of one obstetrician talking to another in horrified tones of the scene of one of her husband's emergency deliveries. "And do you know, Mary, he said there wasn't even a carpet on the floor." A long way from the deliveries we had been called to, with an accumulation of newspapers as bedding, an old sack beside the bed.

As our children grew they developed very differently into four different moulds. Their first year of education had been at the same splendid beginners' class where I used to be pushed in a push-chair. In their turn they announced, "One chap comes in a pram, another on a horse."

This preparatory school had been run by a calm, amused, experienced minister's daughter under the auspices of a missionary college in a sunny garden. A better beginning in courteous and gentle discipline where you learned to keep your feet in life's shallower waters could not be found. The budding missionaries took part in the teaching; they learned the simplicities and complexities of awakening minds, and that must have helped them a lot in their further spheres of work. Later, however, the powers-that-were decided that time spent on Hebrew and Philosophy was more important for the emergent nations, and subsequent children were the losers. Ours, and I myself, are still grateful alumni. We sang "All things bright and beautiful" in the chapel, and that is how they appeared to a child.

At five years old, our children dispersed to different schools that suited them, rather than being confined in one shape. Parents and children still deserve that much choice, although there are times when everyone thinks it is the wrong one. Living where we did, outside interests were easy. Friends lived within bell-pull distance, there were gardens and the river to play in or at, and from a very early age those who had to take buses were independent. One daughter at five began to come home later and later. We discovered that, with her cheap ticket allowing transfer from bus to bus, she was avidly exploring Edinburgh from the upper deck. As in our youth, we had no qualms at children doing this; at that period we used to walk all over the city, often late at night, and never worry. It is tragic that this dream state is shattered now.

The river was an exploring route too. One day we held a Viking's funeral. One of our bantams had developed a secret brood in a leafy corner and, when it was discovered, it was found to be on the back of our hibernating tortoise, who had unfortunately succumbed as his bedclothes had been kicked away. In death he was feather-light. We all climbed the wall, fixed a lighted candle to his back and saluted him as he sailed slowly down to Leith. Swans nested on the riverbank near a factory where the girls used to give them their lunch-bags, and the pen reposed on a mound of crushed paper labelled 'Co-op' while her cob patrolled the waterway. If you walked past in the early morning, she would be standing over the nest, turning her great olive-green eggs while he dibbled nearby. In earlier days, this road was called Puddocky. The milkmaids used it on the way to their herds on the water meadows of Bonnington.

The last concerted part of building in the 'New Town', our crescent had been conceived primarily as a boulevard to lead to Newhaven, parallel to Leith Walk. Appropriate housing had been built higher up the hill for superior social status; 'schoolmasters' were also socially acceptable, and these houses were built for their benefit from 1817 onwards. Early last century, a well-remembered dominie had dwelled there. He is unnamed, but he was one of the earliest to introduce a textbook. Previously, children had sat on their benches and repeated their two languages:

"A bull is jist a he-coo,
Mud is jist glaur."

A few years later, Chopin, shivering and coughing through a damp northern winter, had stayed there for some months, accompanied by George Sand. The Poles instituted a plaque on his house and still revere his anniversary there.

By the river were two barracks, the original meal mills belonging to the Canons of Holyrood, then known as the Rookeries. They were now occupied by the poor in means, in small partitioned rooms, and behind them lay Kate Baxter's Yard. One of these buildings has been 'improved', the second pulled down, and in the demolition, Kate's secrets were revealed. Below the soil, many tiny bones were discovered. She must have been an early child-minder; mortality among infants was high, and proper burial beyond many people's means. The handsome stone commemorating her name for posterity decorates the court of a garage on the site.

While our children grew, we occasionally managed some holidays, but a practice was a hard taskmaster then, and certainly not a moneyed one. A war service gratuity funded one magnificent expedition to Arosa in Switzerland. The children were recovering from whooping-cough and needing to be restored in brilliant snow after a depressingly long wet winter.

Arriving in Basle, from a grey Britain full of slush, we were staggered at the cleanliness everywhere, from the station on-wards — our first sight of electrified railway, instead of steam, smoke and smuts. In the speeding train beside green lake and green river, eating hot croissants and cherry jam for breakfast, we looked out at lines of dazzling washing, and coffee-coloured cows that seemed to have been recently scrubbed. Arriving late at the pension, we were offered an early supper for four children and a helper. "Leider nur vierundzwanzig Eier," the hostess apologised, — alas, only a twenty-four-egg omelette. At home, we were still rationed.

The older ones went out skiing. This was not for my damaged knees, and I walked the snow-trodden paths. In 1950, the sanatoria were still full of tuberculous patients sent to the high, rare air to help their breathing. Those on their feet were sent out for walks, one at a time, thirty feet apart, forbidden to speak to one another, as they needed all their breath for action. It was a macabre illustration, under the early morning sunlight, of Thomas Mann's 'The Magic Mountain'.

In the afternoons, we ate unbelievable cakes — at home it was still dry sponge.

Later, we bought a long cow-and-henhouse in East Lothian with a small legacy and turned it into a cottage. Here we could occasionally snatch a weekend, or spend school holidays. The older children had old bicycles. I had a still older one that creaked along with one of the younger ones on the carrier. Country roads were safe then, and there was a convenient disused aerodrome not far away, on whose runways they could practise their wobbly balance. When Edinburgh's airport was undergoing improvement, this came into commission for a short while, but was not highly organised. I had to fly to London at short notice, and climbed into a plane standing at the ready — it did not seem very big, but no one said me nay.

"This is going to London isn't it? " I asked the steward.

"No Madam, to Wick," was the reply, so back I went to the waiting-room, which seemed to be an old railway coach.

Next door to us at the cottage lived a retired gamekeeper. In the morning, we would see him slowly loping across the field, a spaniel and her four pups spaced out behind him. Behind them came our two youngest, each trying to take steps as long as he did. They made a fine frieze, with a doocot at one end of the field and a herd of cows at the other, who always stood where the sun shone on them, backs to the east in the morning, to the west at night, so the dying rays could warm their rumps. An engineer uncle told me that when the first jet engines were used in aircraft, once the cows were inured to the noise, they used to turn tail on to enjoy the warmth of the plane's take-off!

Our village boasted a smithy, and Alec Ainslie, a man of great kindness and direct blue gaze, always gave the young a welcome if they kept out of hooves' way in the forge. Those times of country living made an immense difference to the children, and gave their friends an escape too; the garden would fill with tents. They held a party in our big living-room with a friend blowing his pipes for the reels. The cows gathered at the windows drawn by the sounds of revelry, and grew annoyed when their heavy breathing clouded their view. Alec made us a bar to prevent their horns dashing the glass.

"You'll want it as high as a stirk's shouther," he said, and it was. They used it regularly, as an itching post.

CONFIDENCES

XXI CINDERELLA YEARS

Once post-war readjustment had been made, medical discontent increased.

Families saw little of the practising parent, and where the mother was involved in acting as extension to the practice, she was too often crabby and hurried. We were lucky in that throughout the children's youth we had been blessed by a series of helpers who really helped, and who were all a good deal more patient than I was. This kept my sanity.

Now that we lived away from the practice, and its mechanics were effectively run by a medical team, I could return to the physiology lab and life with students, which also widened the family horizon. There are great rewards in running a household and watching its development, but one is always running into new questions of thinking and being. The chance to work with different age groups within a scientific discipline and become involved in their emotional difficulties is an education in itself.

In the official buildings of the University, there were no comfortable corners in which to give tutorials, so the budding medicals used to come down to the afternoon fireside and discuss their essays there. This gave them a taste of domesticity which some of them were missing badly. This showed when they would shortly return thinking 'they had left their notes', and then found them after all, but stayed for tea. It also benefited our returning children thus to meet some grown-ups who shared their problems.

Nationalities were distinguishable as the coffee-pot was carried in. An all-Scottish group would sit uneasily in a tight row on the sofa. The English would be sprawled all over the place, some of them leaping to their feet to help with the door. The Africans lounged loosely and happily. The Asians sat suspiciously. It was a little self-donated prize if, by the end of the session, they were all relaxed and talking easily. A bonus was a wet day when a broody mother saw their damp shoes were by the fender and their toes towards the fire. Whatever good it may have done them, it did wonders for me having this contact with an age group other than the nursery.

University life entered a much more interesting period. Many mature students had returned to commence or continue their studies after war service, and the whole situation became more adult. Refugees from war-torn countries began to be accepted, and language difficulties had more to be reckoned with. The University itself had to extend its buildings, its economic sense unfortunately gaining over its artistic hopes. The original plans that would have replaced some very degraded and bug-ridden buildings to the east were abandoned, and douce and beautiful George Square started its ruinous way to becoming skyscrapers of learning. One of the reasons solemnly given to the staff in convocation was that it was 'full of rats'. These fauna are as native to any city as fleas, but not recognised in polite society. They may well yet be there, but probably have the sense to prefer the stone area to concrete. We are left with a surprising muddle in the square, luckily much obscured by the trees in the garden in the middle.

New facilities grew, and so did the undergraduate body which was still eagerly making up for lost time. No longer could a student of medicine spend his days playing bridge, passing the requisite exams at the last possible opportunity. Generally it was a very invigorating time of learning, and the horizon was wide open, or so we thought.

A healthy draught from other quarters blew through the ranks. When the Hungarian uprising took place in 1956, a group of about twenty young men from different faculties in the University settled in a small hut in Princes Street Gardens. Their resolution was to live for two weeks in mid-term, existing on two shillings a day each; any money left over, or collected from sympathetic public, was to go to support any Hungarian refugee students Alma Mater saw fit to admit.

They kept this up faithfully, preserving an ascetic calm and going to early markets for their food so that they might keep up with classes. They all wrote diaries, which, since they were physiologically interesting, they kindly consigned to me for editing. The chief memories from these were the relative lengths of time that dreams of sex and food continued. As I remember, sex started to take a back seat from eight to ten days, but yearnings for Mars Bars continued longer.

The night of their release, they all came down to the house for supper. We had prepared a lot of fresh fruit and veg. and protein, from all of which restricted finance had disqualified them, but it was remarkable how little they ate or drank: even in that short time, the stomach appears to shrink.

There was an interesting young Indian among their number who against paternal desires had supped deep of socialist principles. From his home in the north, he had journeyed overland to Russia, averring that his Hindi had been understood nearly to the gates of Moscow. From there, he had crossed Finland, continued west to Bergen, and there taken a boat to Newcastle. He maintained that certain Norwegians were not allowed ashore as they had contracted V.D. In fact, he had misheard; it was T.B. Thus may rumour so easily raise its head and disseminate its misinterpretations.

In his youth he had spent much time studying yoga, and the disciplines of living on a reduced diet had not given him the same distress as his more robust colleagues. His occupation in this country was to study the artificial insemination of cattle, to improve many of the sacred skeletons that roamed his native streets. I hope he has been lucky.

The following year, it is a pleasure to record, the University opened its doors to 'homeless' Hungarians. We had several of them in the medical faculty, and admirable students they proved to be.

A PICTURE OF HEALTH

Universities never belie their name, if constitutionally or financially possible. Twenty-three years earlier the son of a German mother and an Austrian father, then a Professor in the University of Heidelberg, came to Edinburgh after a year's study of chemistry in Innsbruck and a period of caring for experimental rats in the physiology department at Cambridge. Medical training was barred to him in his own country, and he hoped to study here. He was interviewed by the Edinburgh Dean, Professor Sidney Smith, who produced a flowery invitation to the medical faculty of Edinburgh from his home university of Heidelberg for the celebration of its four hundredth birthday.

"What is the thought behind this? " asked the Dean.

"The programme as planned will demonstrate that Cancer and Mental Defect have been eliminated by the Third Reich," was the reply. The Dean went off, leaving the hopeful immigrant wriggling in his chair. After an hour he came back.

"My colleagues and I," he said, "feel that the best reply we can make to this invitation is to take one of Heidelberg's displaced sons into the medical faculty and give him his training."

Such was knowledge married to wisdom − and Jim has never forgotten it.

Primary care, represented by the functions of the family doctor, deals with nine tenths of the medical load. Since the advent of the National Health Act, the perceived medical demand was in danger of swamping the personnel to the detriment of patient and practitioner. This was reaching the point where the doctors were desperate and the patients despairing. It became essential for the doctors to restore their idealism and morale, to form a coherent group, to refocus on their medical and post-graduate needs and not only on the new administration and finance.

In 1953, a founding group of like-minded doctors came together to form the College of General Practitioners. Dr John Hunt (the late Lord Hunt of Fawley) had some remarkable tales to tell of his battles with the London fraternity of specialist Colleges. They considered this a decline in their dignity. However, the seedling flourished and in 1964 attained its Royal Charter.

It brought together a group of thinkers alike in purpose and ideals of practice and developed courses of post-graduate meetings and further education all over the country. Family doctors had often worked in solitude with little time to study further developments in their craft, and too often their work was unacknowledged and denigrated by the hospitals which are still slow in recognising the immense load carried by primary care. The coming together of fellow professionals, ruggedly individual as many of them were, and the inclusion at some of the meetings of medical ancillary workers, became a source of strength. The profession began attending to its own health: the physician began healing himself.

Slowly the atmosphere grew less tense. The doctor himself may not be so obsessional, but he is more interested and interesting. The patient is asking for more information, is getting it, and is better served by a less remote and exhausted fraternity. Both parties are beginning to work together. The autocratic home doctor of my youth would now rightly be questioned, and his great moustache might well quiver at what he would consider as impertinence. We were brought up on the dictum that curiosity killed the cat. Now posturing paternalism is on its way out.

Those who sigh for the good old bedside manner as they sit on their waiting-room chairs do not recognise that pain was considered salutary then and that little was done for its relief, that medicine was considered best when beastly to taste, that the doctor in many cases would only come if you paid him, unless you were Panel, or Poor Law. They have little knowledge of the strains of living in the underbelly of society out of reach of medical treatment, although new horrors of disease appear to develop as rapidly as we overcome the old ones.

In the Thirties, hospitals were as overcrowded as nowadays, and far more understaffed. In huge uncurtained open wards, forty patients might be perched simultaneously on cold metal bedpans, with only a screen at the door, which might be pushed aside by Houseman or Chief in a hurry.

There is more dignity now in personal life − but the patient whizzes in and out of hospital at such high speed that he misses some of the lessons of tolerance that his predecessors learned, and he does not get a chance to learn the faces of those who care for him, to build up a two-way relationship.

Formerly, the Ward Sister was the hostess, and the confidante.

She knew the patient, the patient knew his nurses, and many of his fellow inmates, frequently worse off than himself. In acute conditions, these lessons are rare. The ward cleaner is now often the one who will take the time to listen and to nod; the visiting student is often too busy looking up his medical symptomatic directory. On two occasions when I have been a patient myself, I never discovered who the Sister was.

Only the chronically ill, too often segregated in their own group, teach survival by their example and still retain their sense of fun. They have reached full maturity in coping with infirmity. "Death is no problem," said one, "but living certainly is."

The College of General Practitioners began for the faithful few. Ideas grow slowly, and professionals tend to hug their hard earned prejudices.

In the early Sixties, the face of family medicine was still clouded, and it looked as if general practice was going to disintegrate entirely. Its practitioners were an ageing group, the newcomers rarely coming into it with a positive attitude, but rather with a certain resentment, many having failed their specialist entry. Unfortunately, this atmosphere was encouraged by the more limited hospital outlooks, and it did not make for happy relations between the two sections, institutional and domestic. Morale reached rock bottom, and the general practice services were murmuring in terms of striking, partly because of income differences, partly on account of general discontent at their workload.

Whitehall bureaucracy used its well-tried bright idea, setting up the Fraser Committee to examine the shortcomings and frustrations of the National Health Service. Medical representatives, of whom my husband was one, gathered at the Elephant and Castle in London, and evidence was sought from groups of family doctors throughout the country. Some of these meetings were fairly civilised, some downright awful. Colleagues were so disheartened that their understanding failed to function, and their reception of the proposals in meetings crowded into halls and lecture theatres was that of baying undergraduates, or the House of Commons on a bad day. Certainly no bedside, or other manners were discernible: the observer came away shattered.

CINDERELLA YEARS

For two years these deliberations continued. Then good fortune produced the appointment in 1964 of a really effective Minister of Health, Kenneth Robinson. He held all the humanity, rather than just the dogma, that the title implies, and, moreover, was prepared to listen. His father had been a general practitioner, so he had inside knowledge. He accepted four nominations from the profession, representing the United Kingdom, along with members of the B.M.A. secretariat, and appointed a complementary group of civil servants. There were frequent impasses and eventually the whole situation looked so worrying that the 'four wise men of general practice' were incarcerated for some days at an unpublished address, incommunicado. The rest of us sat tensely waiting. Would white smoke or black rise from the chimney? Victory and sense, or defeat and chaos? On emerging, they met their government opposite numbers and together they thrashed out a final joint solution, the General Practitioners' Charter, its implementation to be negotiated laboriously between 1964 and 1966.

The essence of this was that the general practitioner was to be paid for being a doctor, rather than a dogsbody; he was to have the support of nurses who were to be nurses, receptionists who were to be receptionists, secretaries who were to be secretaries. General medical practice was encouraged to group itself into a team combining in its work — not separate professionals stuffing inadequate notes into bursting envelopes, nurses having to make the tea, explain to patients, and soothe everybody's temper, and wives rushing to the phone while the milk boiled over. They could now relax a little, develop their own initiatives, or be the wives they had set out to be. In short, it was a potential system where all parties had a chance to do the work for which they had had a long and arduous training. It was a new and natural vista in patient care and communication.

Full development of this idea was understandably slow. Professionals dig into their shells like timid hermit crabs and deplore change, stonewalling the simple and obvious, such as changing the envelopes provided for patients' notes into shapes that fit their contents and standard filing cabinets, or setting up appointments systems. Inaccessibility can so easily become part of a mystique; many doctors had long ago evolved their own systems, largely hieroglyphic. However, the atmosphere began to change, slowly and suspiciously at first, but with a new generation beginning to yearn for efficiency it speeded up, and the general practitioner actually began to perceive that he too had a home life that was responsive.

Since those years of depression, it has been deeply satisfying to watch this progress develop. Eager and intelligent young graduates, now needing yet further training in their own speciality, are seeking entry into the privileged service of dealing with people against their own background. It has developed a rich growth of understanding and commitment. The Cinderella years are nearly over, but in the overcrowded areas bursting with fluctuating populations of different beliefs and languages, there is yet a long way to go.

The medical team should now be the norm, consisting of nurses, health visitors, social workers and helpers who are willing to help the aged and infirm with all aspects of living, in their homes if possible.

One day, a busload of Japanese arrived to visit my husband's practice, one of the pioneer examples of this team ideal. At the gate they met a health visitor.

"How many beds do you cover? " asked the leader.

"About twenty-one thousand," was the reply.

They were left looking vainly for the building that could house these numbers.

DESIGN FOR A

COMMITTEE

XXII   OTHER PLACES, OTHER JOBS

Family living is a schizophrenic occupation. Periods of frenzied
activity alternate with an empty house; the post brings cheques,
or the purse is flat; there is food in the kitchen, or the cupboard
is bare — it all adds to the excitement, and one learns to
manoeuvre with leftovers, of time, cash or food. As a family
grows, the individual lives bud out in unforeseen directions like so
many octopus arms, and bring back so many variations into a one-
track professional house that the mind boggles, but fortunately
ticks on.

Twenty-one years of University activity held some alternatives
for me. For a period, involvement in its General Council, a sort of
mini-parliament of assorted graduates, gave glimpses of the con-
volutions of Academia.   One of the most teasing exercises was
reading through the curricula of various departments from which
the prospective student was supposed to glean the needs of his
academic future, but which were more likely to lose him in a
jungle of verbiage.   Law and Theology were the worst. The sug-
gestion that the Department of English Language should
undertake the formidable task of rewriting them more clearly was,
unfortunately for aspiring students, outvoted.

In those days, the authorities produced a very good free tea
preceding the meetings, to which we often came ravening after an
afternoon's teaching. In the Senate Room it was interesting to
see the higher echelons make a run for the fancy cakes; presum-

ably plain living and high thinking was the rule at home. When the Minutes (so misnamed) of the last meeting became interminable, we could look across the road at the second-floor windows of a dancing-school, where stout gentlemen were being introduced to the tango and the quickstep by gallant young ladies in black. Alternatively, we had some fine portraits by Raeburn and others of the thinkers who had gone before. One, surprisingly, seems to have taught in his nightcap.

Later, I became involved in a national committee with a wider remit, backed by the Rowntree Trust. Its aim was to prophesy the directions and needs of the University in a Changing World. The changes were faster than we could keep up with, but for the few years we met in various milieux from hotels to student hostels, they were certainly interesting. 'We' consisted of two University principals, a mixed bag of dons, two research men, and a secretary: my role could best be described as a common denominator.

In hotels, we often crossed the paths of other gatherings. Once in Bloomsbury we encountered a large group of pre-adolescent moppets of both sexes who were engaged in 'Come Dancing' trials. Little girls in curlers, with reddened finger-nails, came down to breakfast in fancy bedroom-slippers − perhaps their feet were sore − and joined little boys with smarmed-down hair, all with their eager mothers. I carry a cherished memory of a bewildered teacher of Classics picking his way among various ironing-boards on the landings, where the maternal contingent was busy pressing acres of net skirts in blinding colours.

Many of our meetings became so involved in jargon and the continual use of the unfortunate word 'Elitist', which always sounds like an advertisement for soft-centred chocolates or hair-dressing establishments, that I felt my presence was unjustified, and said so. However, in those circles, you may only say so in a 'paper'. I gave my reasons thus at the next meeting. The interesting result was that half my colleagues came up to say that they couldn't understand cross-faculty jargon either, and thereafter we all debated in more straightforward terms.

Meetings in London are usually bedevilled by the local commuter. He arrives late and leaves early; work can only be got through by ordering lunch at the conference table, and getting on with the job between bites at a sandwich. Provincial venues were therefore more valuable, and in some we had to do some unofficial trouble-shooting with agitated student groups. One of the most successful was in a large pub where a busty, brassy blonde did a lot of elegant handiwork on a deficient piano. The students' main objection was that the new university women's hostels had had shaving points built into their bedrooms, while the men had none. As most of the arguers were bearded, we wondered whether this had a personal bias. At last, they accepted the fact that universities attempt to reimburse themselves by letting out their hostels in the vacation to conferences, that this facility was a good selling point to businessmen used to their comforts, and a help in boosting academic central finances. The budding, and too often the flourishing male intellectual tends to tunnel vision, or a vista of the flat earth. Now that he often does the washing up and even helps with the delivery of his own baby, he is improving.

Meanwhile, my husband, while still conducting a busy general practice with his partners, was commuting to London twice weekly to work on central medical policies. This meant two consecutive nights in a railway sleeper and straight on to work in the morning, but later, air travel gave a chance of more nights in his bed. When Edinburgh was served by a smaller airport, fetching him held its delays. In winter, one might sit listening to the tannoy announcing that owing to fog, snow, too much water on the runway, or violent gales, the plane was diverted elsewhere. Elsewhere usually meant Glasgow, and the passengers were then bussed back to their home base some hours later, cold and tired.

Later on, official life produced ceremonial dinners that had to be attended. Along with the cocktail party, these are surely the nadir of entertainment, and the high table is rarely a feast of reason, or, for that matter, food. Stuffed evening shirts, unless well wined, usually let their irritation show, and civic dignitaries are rarely natural sparklers. However, certain occasions glow.

There were three lovely Lord Mayors. One was a cabinet-maker who had helped to build the beautiful coaches of the Brighton Belle. One was a nurse, an admirable woman firmly called Lord Mayor, her husband being her Consort, and one a very interesting

Church of England parson who also drove a fork-lift truck for British Leyland, to get nearer to what he considered his groundwork to be. All these modest people continued to take part in their professions in any way they could, before going on to their civic duties every day. Once we attended a dinner in the Grocers' Hall in the City of London, the Grocers all wearing sables and quite remote from the shelves of the supermarket. You shook salt and pepper out of silver camels, in memory of Marco Polo and his spice train. There were further dinners with other Royal Colleges in London, followed by a mad rush to the station in full evening-dress for the night train north, and work in the morning.

After twenty-one years in the classroom, I became a minor cog in genetic research. The early study of chromosomes involved a search for their relevant genes, and a connection was being sought into the possible heredity of congenital malformation. For cellular investigation, samples of blood from the parents were needed, and after groundwork on birth, obstetric history and relationships, these had to be collected. This entailed travel by road or rail, driving to the Borders or the involved conurbations of Strathclyde, and training and bussing to the far north. The blood samples had to be fresh, and occasionally shared a refrigerator in a small hotel wrapped up beside the next day's dinner. A letter was sent to the person concerned, describing what was at stake, with a stamped addressed envelope for reply; a letter also went to their general practitioner so, if puzzled, they could discuss it. It is to the immense credit of the patients that, out of about a hundred and fifty letters, there was only one refusal.

True, my reception was not always welcoming. A lady on a Glasgow stairhead stood and screamed at her door. However, eventually realising that her neighbours would be agog, she let me in, and beside her fire with strong tea and her skirt comfortably rolled up to show knickered knees, she grew interested in what the whole exercise was about and produced a brawny arm with a vein in it for tapping.

An old fisherman in Fraserburgh gave details of wartime shipwreck in his kitchen while his wife used winkles to bait his line coiled beside her in a circular tub. A forester near Fort William, a depressed mother with three child deaths in the Tweed valley, all grew interested in the fact that we were were interested in them, and that their experience might be of use to others. It was an amazing display of generosity. They all received a letter of thanks, and what information could be given on our findings. These eventually proved more negative than we expected, but everyone had helped.

A small exercise involved a look at the distribution of women in medicine. This was in the 1960's, a different picture from today. The women graduates early in the century had had to meet fierce challenges from their teachers, and their fellow students. With iron determination they had climbed high in some specialties, more so than in the generation looked at. Was the answer in their single-mindedness? True, they came from a period when domestic concerns were somebody else's — a mother, sister, maiden aunts or servants — and frequently their profession was the sole taskmaster.

Later generations married earlier and had to care for their children before their profession: climbing back on the ladder after precious years lost is strenuous. Now, with the help of the Pill, women plan their confinements for vacation or immediately post-examination. One of these appearing for her viva in midwifery bulging with her eight month pregnancy was confronted by her examiner standing in the middle of the room. He took a chair from the wall, firmly sat down on it himself, and gave her a grilling while she stood like a defaulter before him. Was he one of the architects of what was euphemistically termed 'The Outcome of Pregnancy Committee'? About twenty years earlier the first committee on contraception had been convened, consisting entirely of learned gentlemen.

Within a few months of their graduation, you meet these young women pushing a pram. They are very good at it, but the challenges are different, the arrangements with their husbands remarkable. Wild young men whom you knew in the early student years are suddenly to be seen carrying bags bulging with groceries and are well versed in washing-powder technology.

It is never easy. An eminent Chief for whom I worked and whom I held in the greatest respect eventually attained a professorial chair. She used to sigh for a domestic background. "Oh, if only I had a wife," she said, as she used to dash back from the lab to cook, decant, host and serve her friends an evening meal. It is a lesson in flexibility. I wonder if a Working Women's Union will ever make its way to the top table of the T.U.C.

All my women bosses, in hospital, surgical theatre, and laboratory, were superb taskmistresses, and I salute their memories with gratitude and respect.

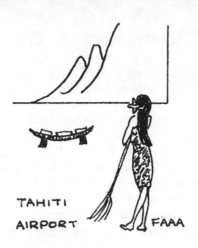

TAHITI
AIRPORT   FAAA

XXIII   TRAVELLING

Early in the Seventies, my husband was appointed as a travelling professor for a series of commitments overseas, some of which I could share. A spectator view is always a privilege, and swithers between amazement and amusement.

We started off at a conference in Tel Aviv. Israel was remarkable for its good-looking and superbly fit youth, both sexes in Army uniform, relaxedly carrying guns. We were entertained rather oddly by a mixed choir of very neat pubescent schoolchildren, all wearing long white socks. Under their conductor, in English, they entertained us with "I can't give you anything but love — babee". This was followed by a dramatic actress declaiming in Hebrew. She then obligingly translated it for us, the rules of Exodus: life for life, eye for eye, tooth for tooth, hand for hand, foot for foot, burning for burning. The listener's blood ran cold. Next day we saw Sephardic Jews in their long black coats and sidelocks being hustled off by police. They had been attempting to bomb a shop called the Eros Boutique.

We shared College proceedings in both Canada and Australia. Both were very grand, and intensely serious, the grandees in gowns and bullion, behaving like well-turned-out men of the cloth. We arrived in Canada the morning after a parliamentary election, to see deflated balloons and litter lying about the hotel ballroom floor, in the tired light of day. Was it for this that the carillon of the Houses of Parliament used to play several verses of "Hark the

A PICTURE OF HEALTH

Herald Angels Sing" at seven o'clock on a May morning?

I flew down to Charlottesville for the medical graduation of a nephew. Jefferson's beautiful cloistered parallelogram, full of grass, trees and birds, was crowded with parents. Down the centre in academic groups marched the new graduates, who, after the usual splendid platitudes from the Chancellor, took off their mortarboards and threw them into the air, like hundreds of gay kites. The final year medical students had endowed an award to the most helpful member of their faculty. It was a delight to see a round and smiling little woman in pink receive it. She was a pathology technician, who had manned her microscope and helped them round the clock.

In Australia, meetings took place in a vast building in Melbourne with several halls, and on each occasion two parties of gentlemen each carrying a small case, crossed the foyer to go in opposite directions. One lot held the gowns and mortarboards of Australian medicine, the others, presumably, the aprons and other paraphernalia necessary to Australian Freemasonry. They all stayed studiously apart. Years later, in a students' hostel during vacation, the same situation arose, when three different groups were meeting. Three tables in the dining-hall were labelled Social Sciences, Telephone Samaritans, Telecommunications. There appeared to be no mutual language, and communicating smiles were nervous, as we passed in the corridors.

Crossing the Pacific via the exotic airport of Tahiti, we visited our elder son and his family in Peru where, in the high Andes, we confronted medical sights only previously seen in old textbooks.

On the homeward journey, the airport at Bogota produced delays. Thanks to a tough Scots engineer with a figure like a rock, the aeroengineers remobilised our plane. We waited for eight hours while a Colombian official with the manners of a high church canon reverently gave us each a dry bun and two packets of Colombian coffee as a pacifier.

Back in Europe, we had medical visits that were more reassuring, comparing the facilities in primary care of the Netherlands, Germany, Austria, Switzerland, Italy, Scandinavia and Finland. Some were authoritarian, some full of laissez faire; some apparently forgot that most of us can be sick, and needing their

196

care. Some were well run on insurance schemes, some seemed governed by the rattle of cash registers. Some were very conscious of status: large advertisements painted on house walls of the speciality dealt with within, or the availability of the treatment considered up to the minute — my husband opened a door labelled PHYSIOTHERAPIE to reveal a broom cupboard — a shot in the locker for Women's Lib?

We always met kindness, courtesy, a flood of information, interest, and occasionally patronage. Some countries still consider specialisation of some sort essential to the kudos of the practitioner, and, where patients do their own 'medical shopping', presumably this makes it far simpler for them.

In Finland we stayed in an hotel overshadowed by the Russian presence; the swimming-pool and sauna apparently opened only for their arrival. Outside was a signpost marked Leningrad, x Km. We had a four day tour among lakes, modern churches, cities blinking after months of winter, above flower-markets ablaze with tulips, daffodils, crocus, every form of spring blossom pushing its way at once, while many fields were golden with dandelions. Perhaps they were used for salad. Every city has a Sibelius memorial.

The real goodbye to winter was the sauna. Each lake had a bathhouse, a square cottage at the waterside with its smoking Saturday chimney. Our hotel gave us this privilege, and Jim and I were beckoned in by an enormous beaming lady, who called us Pappi and Mammi, giving us each a towel about a foot square. It seemed to be intended for mopping the face, as its dimensions were useless elsewhere. We lay on red hot planks, were sloshed with tepid water, and heated up again. Then she opened a door, gave us a friendly push, and lo, we were swimming in the ice-water lake among the swans, with a man mowing his grass a few feet away, quite uninterested. The feeling of invigoration was fantastic.

After reheating, we were laid on a further wooden slab and thoroughly loofahed all over, between the toes and elsewhere, finished off with splashing buckets of tepid water. Weakened, we towelled and dressed, but once complete, felt in a state of levitation of body and spirit. Walking up the path through the wood to a delicious dinner, we felt ready to be welcomed by St.

A PICTURE OF HEALTH

Peter at the gate. A student's hostel in Helsinki was the best designed I have ever seen, and, in vacation, entirely manned by its occupants, beautiful and courteous, each student T-shirt decorated with a large sun.

Our final visit, in 1978, was to Egypt, where the greatest contrasts were. This was a Government-sponsored visit, and we met officials. Their medical men found much to admire in British general practice and hoped for a similar training for their graduates. Only the best examinees were admitted from school to medicine, and their intelligence was very high indeed. Their textbooks are all in English, and their knowledge wide rather than deep, the wisdom developed in contact with patients restricted by the enormous clinics, so that their bedside experience is scant. Following graduation, they are directed either to the Army, or to distant villages on the Nile's green length. There, they may live a very isolated life for two years, away from their peers and the chance of extending medical knowledge, serving the fellahin. Naturally, they long for the fleshpots of Cairo and Alexandria.

The Minister of Health was very aware of this problem. He said that infection by Bilharzia was so general that the only chance they had to treat it was when men were in military service, under directions. Seeing the very varied use of the canals, we did not find this news surprising, fishing, washing, camel-swilling and other activities being freely carried on there. I met a woman doctor in Public Health whose remit was the care of over a million Cairene schoolgirls. There were several women in the medical groups we met, but they always automatically sat in the back rows, and kept silent except when approached. In the front, with folded arms, many decorations, and looking remarkably like Rameses, sat a medical chief of the Army, who never opened his mouth.

In the medical outposts, hospitality was always the first issue, tea, coffee or coke—the courtesy of natural hosts.

Each patient paid a fee, then three drachmas, the purchasing equivalent of 1½ cigarettes. Free medicine was not considered curative. Midwifery was conducted in the home by a midwife; contraceptive pills available, occasionally collected by the men, and condoms could be obtained too. The patients and their families squatted quietly outside in heat and dust, the transport camels and donkeys patiently waiting like a crowd of country buses.

Egyptian doctors loved statistics and format, and drew beautiful coloured diagrams. The Arab world, cradle of mathematics, still believed in them. I was told by a neurological surgeon newly returned from Japan that there the norm was 1.26 children!

There was a great love of children. We saw them carried astride their fathers' shoulders to avoid the suffocating crush on the pavements: there was always a feeling of kindness.

Succumbing to a chest infection in a drab hotel bedroom while my companions left the city on further visits, I was tended by enormous chambermen—all servants were male. They knew I had no baksheesh, a necessary perquisite, but could not have been gentler, advancing to put tender hands on my hot brow, and intoning "Madaaame." There was not an atom of familiarity in this behaviour, only a genuine concern of the moment, and they brought me trays of orange juice and toast at intervals. One had an active cockroach on it, but they did not regard this as untoward, so neither did I.

The men prayed wherever they were, five times a day, facing Mecca. On reaching Heathrow, I spotted three Arab backs, two men and a boy, kneeling with their heads in a corner, watched by two airport officials. One said, "They should be facing the east."

"It shouldn't be allowed," said the other.

XXIV   LOOKING BACK

History is much more of a reality to the old than to the young. Learning off a row of recurrent Kings and their dates is about as helpful as reading the "Begats" in the Bible, unless you have the King James version in Pidgin English. There the book of Chronicles reads, "I bilong Elkanab, him bilong Jeroboam, him bilong Mahath . . ." When you are old, you find you bilong to a great many interesting people, and begin to be historical to your grandchildren.

History is about people, and you find yourself as a connecting thread. In one lifetime, the changes amaze!

In my childhood, as we walked the streets of the poorer quarters of Edinburgh, we saw conditions as normal that would pull up any passer-by nowadays. The old were bowed, shuffling along in splayed shoes, their smelling clothes often soaked through, their mumbling toothless jaws suddenly widening in a wild cackle. Yet they rarely lost their wit, though there was little to be witty about.

The middle-aged might show the bowed legs, the pigeon-chests, the knobbed skulls of infantile rickets, the curved spines of tuberculosis, the dragging shrivelled limbs of poliomyelitis, sometimes shackled by enormous metal splints and an ugly raised boot to match one limb with another. The limbless rarely had any replacement at all, perhaps a peg leg replacing the amputation following accident or war injury, a hook replacing a hand.

LOOKING BACK

The children might be pale and grizzling, wearing layers of adherent clothing, and often unshod. They had the yellow gum of eternal colds around their mouths and noses, and faced a row of ferocious infectious diseases yet to come, with their after-effects delaying their attack for later life. There were the eternal penalties of overcrowding: bugs, fleas, impetigo, scabies, erysipelas, recurrent diarrhoeas, and the inheritance of venereal disease from their progenitors. Little children might be seen on crutches, like the last boy following the Pied Piper of Hamelin. When, in the city, did we last see a Long John Silver?

In my childhood, first treatment was home-made, and practical; the doctor cost MONEY. When your throat was sore, you were made to gargle with salt, or Condy's fluid, and spit furiously. Condy's fluid was more interesting as you spat pink, but salt was cheaper. If that didn't sort it, you had your tonsils painted with stinging tannin. If your chest hurt, it was either rubbed with warm oil, or poulticed with a burning bread mush that cooled rapidly, or you sat with a towel over your head breathing deeply at the spout of a sort of china kettle, full of fuming decongestant. An aching ear received a hot onion in it, or warm oil, and you laid it throbbing, on a hot water bottle if you were stylish enough to possess a rubber one. If there was further inflammation, leeches might be applied, like rich black slugs. An alternative poultice was a worn sock round the neck, said to be efficacious if it was your own, and unwashed. Whatever illness you had, recovery was a long and tedious battle that your body had to fight. There were no 'instant' drugs.

If you bled, and cold water would not stop it, someone fetched a spider's web, which helped to clot the bleeding. If you ate what you shouldn't, you were given a strong drench of kitchen salt, so you brought it up again. If you seized up, there were various drastic doses available, but it is worth noting that some infant remedies contained mercurials. The children were found to develop 'Pink Disease' with rosy colouring on palms and soles, and great irritability; only in the forties was this traced to mercury poisoning in their 'opening medicine'.

If your teeth ached, and there was a hole, the remedy was to tie the tooth by a length of string to the doorhandle, and slam the door. The outcome was usually a yell rather than a removal, and oil of cloves which acted as an anti-irritant might be tried. Failing that, a dreaded visit to the dentist: money again.

There were two interesting industrial assets. Men working with machines often damaged their hands, but these tended to heal quicker than expected. Heavy oil had a healing base to it. Similarly, the cellarmen working in the stores in Leith just above sea level where wines were maturing in a cool temperature used to pull the mould off the stone arches to put on any wound, with a satisfactory result. This mould is now known as a first cousin of streptomycin.

When I was working as a nurse, a dressing had to be changed on a tuberculous hip with an open sinus, which had developed a secondary infection. On removal of the gauze, a large bluebottle flew out, and I had a fierce rocket from Sister who implied that I had introduced it. It had left its maggots there, but we discovered they had cleaned the wound entirely of secondary infection. Some years later, in the Spanish Civil War, Trueta the surgeon discovered that encircling a wound entirely in a plaster of Paris gave it a period of immobility where automatic healing processes could progress without interference, much on the principle of a septic tank.

Inoculation, vaccines, and the antibiotic era have brought a total change in the cruder aspects of medicine, ensured the future of many who were crippled early in their lives, and brought about a reduction in pain and tragedy that is quite astounding.

The early pioneers need far greater credit than they receive; those who gave us a safe water supply and effective drainage, brought us easy light and heat, produced easy-to-wash-and-dry laundry, and, most noticeably, cleaned our air. Smoke pollution was a bugbear, and the upheavels of spring-cleaning were a constant reminder. Auld Reekie was only perceivable from Arthur's Seat through a series of veils, heavily perfumed by the breweries at its base. It is said that the young Princesses Elizabeth and Margaret Rose when in residence at Holyrood House complained of this smell; they did not have it in any of their other houses.

"No, said their father, "but there you haven't a mountain

outside your back garden either."

In the Midlands, the dark satanic mills belched smoke and fumes so low on damp days that traffic was reduced to a crawl, and pedestrians coughed their way along black and sticky pavements. It was said that you went through three clean collars a day in Manchester, and bronchitis was *the* national disease. Now you may lift your head, see across the city, and walk with pleasure, if the traffic permits. The national disease is still with us, but compounded by smoking, rather than smoke.

What we have gained is immeasurable in positive health.

The scientific researchers have given us chemotherapy, vaccines, antibiotics, radiotherapy, dialysis, surgical transplants and microsurgery, while the biotechnicians have contributed amazing substitute limbs and organs. The Disabled Olympics now give a dazzlingly swift display of sports among amputees.

The nation's infants are the proof of our advance. Returning to this country from less privileged areas is a startling revelation of our alert and rosy young. Their grannies are changing too, and seem a whole generation younger than those we knew. In the Thirties, those of the 60-plus age group would not have gone swimming and jogging, joined Yoga, or started as members of the Open University. The real and awful poverty that we knew has had a face-lift, although that is not cure.

In my seven decades of world-watching, medicine has assumed an entirely new technical face. Is that face any kinder? Time appears to be an object to overtake, not to appreciate, and we forget its value as a maturing process. Rushed through childhood and processed by education, we relax with the coloured wares of the advertisers, unable to see where we are bamboozled. New drugs, new professions, new experts are constantly spawned, and we are supposed to understand them all. One longs for the old wise woman of the fairytale, or the granny who made the strong tea to support all subjects after a difficult confinement—for comfort.

Why can the so-called caring professions not share their early training in Common Sense? High-tech medicine is useless without good nursing: the memories of illness are simple ones. The sick are unaware of the computer assessing their metabolism, but are utterly thankful for the cool bed, the visitor who will sit and listen or discuss, who will squeeze a little reassurance in their hand. This may be the ward cleaner, another patient, the nurse, the house doctor, the specialist, but it is the most valuable part of health service in the fullest sense. We need contact with *someone* we can trust, not some *thing*. This is very difficult to find in our enormous institutions of healing.

Our younger son who, as a student, met medicine in the United States, Europe and East Africa, and practised as a doctor in Zambia, South Africa and Australia, has chosen to come home where he considers the patient's care is much safer. He practises in the area where his father delivered and cared for three generations. He recognises the same needs.

But his life is a very different one. Ups and downs, joys and frustrations there are, but fewer of the blinding pressures that distort judgement — shortage of time and money. He need no longer be a 24-hour-a-day man. He can see his family, plan his holidays, meet his friends reliably, and keep up to date with his craft. He can be a father to his children, and his wife can pursue her own medical career, part-time, without strain. He is spared the horrible need to send bills to patients who cannot afford to pay them, yet by which he has to live. All these changes have been hammered out by the unrelenting work of his predecessors.

Looking back, I now realise that our best teachers all along were our supporting families, loving and generous, and the never-ending patience of our patients as we learned our craft. One of our grand-daughters is about to start her medical career. I wonder what awaits her? I hope the motto of the Royal College of General Practitioners, "Cum Scientia Caritas", will guard her steps.